Praise for *The Price of Citizenship*

"An instant classic. *The Price of Citizenship* is the first comprehensive examination of the attack on welfare . . . remarkably powerful and richly detailed."
—PAUL ROSENBERG, *The Denver Post*

"Comprehensive and detailed . . . Katz covers the welfare state in all its breadth and along the way, he deploys a truly impressive wealth of relevant knowledge. Even readers with quite different beliefs will find plenty to commend."
—CLIVE COOK, *The National Journal*

"Katz, the dean of our social welfare historians, shows here that a new and troubling vision has come to dominate social policy in recent years. This story needs to be told, and no one tells it better, and with more authority, than Katz."
—EDWARD D. BERKOWITZ,
author of *America's Welfare State:
From Roosevelt to Reagan*

"Rich, compelling . . . Without preaching, Katz meticulously reveals the folly of emulating disintegrative forces rather than balancing them. This is a masterpiece of contemporary history."
—*Publishers Weekly* (starred review)

"Katz is the preeminent historian of poverty in the U.S. today and his new book is essential reading for everyone who wants to understand where we are headed."
—KATHERINE S. NEWMAN,
author of *No Shame in My Game:
The Working Poor in the Inner City*

"A balanced masterpiece of modern history . . . *The Price of Citizenship* is essential reading for anyone concerned about the fate of the American welfare state."
—STEVEN ROBERT ALLEN,
The Weekly Alibi (Albuquerque)

THE PRICE OF CITIZENSHIP

THE PRICE OF CITIZENSHIP

REDEFINING THE AMERICAN WELFARE STATE

MICHAEL B. KATZ

An Owl Book

Henry Holt and Company

New York

Henry Holt and Company, LLC
Publishers since 1866
115 West 18th Street
New York, New York 10011

Henry Holt® is a registered trademark
of Henry Holt and Company, LLC.

The prologue to this book is a condensation
of an article coauthored by Michael B. Katz and Lorrin R. Thomas,
"The Invention of 'Welfare' in America," published
in the *Journal of Policy History,* 1998.

Library of Congress Cataloging-in-Publication Data
Katz, M. B.
    The price of citizenship : redefining the American welfare state / Michael B. Katz.—1st ed.
        p.   cm.
    Includes index.
    ISBN 0-8050-6929-1 (pbk.)
    1. Public welfare—United States—History.   2. Welfare state.   3. United States—Social
policy—History.   I. Title.
HV91 .K37   2001
361.6'5'0973—dc21   00-046906

Henry Holt books are available for special promotions and premiums.
For details contact: Director, Special Markets.

First published in hardcover in 2001 by Metropolitan Books

First Owl Books Edition 2002

DESIGNED BY FRITZ METSCH

Printed in the United States of America
1   3   5   7   9   10   8   6   4   2

TO THE MEMORY OF

GEORGE J. KATZ

(1913–1999)

CONTENTS

THE INVENTION OF WELFARE

In 1950 the British sociologist T. H. Marshall described the triumph of the welfare state as "the subordination of market price to social justice." In recent decades that trajectory has been reversed. While the tension between capitalism and equality remains as powerful as ever, today it is social justice that is subordinate to market price.

Welfare once signified a broad and progressive program with wide public support; the welfare state embodied a generation's hopes and aspirations for universal economic security and protection from the worst consequences of life's ordinary hazards. But by the 1960s this meaning of *welfare* and *welfare state* had changed completely. No longer understood to protect everyone against risk, "welfare" had become a code word for public assistance given mainly to unmarried mothers, mostly young women of color, under Aid to Families with Dependent Children. No other public benefits carried the stigma of welfare. The political left, right, and center all attacked it. In the early 1990s, when President Bill Clinton promised to "end welfare as we know it," everyone knew that he meant AFDC—the most disliked public program in America.

Thus it was not surprising that most of the country—eight out of ten Americans—applauded when Clinton honored his pledge to "end welfare" by signing the 1996 welfare reform bill. In practical terms, the bill ended the sixty-year-old entitlement of the poorest Americans to public assistance, put time limits on benefits, tied aid closely to work, transferred the authority to set benefits and administer programs from the federal government to the states, and greatly reduced or eliminated eligibility for legal immigrants and the disabled.

The new legislation signaled the victory of three great forces—the war on dependence, the devolution of public authority, and the application of market models to public policy— that redefined not only welfare but all of America's vast welfare state. The story of how these forces transformed public policy is important not only because the welfare state consumes a large share of the nation's income and influences the life of every American. It is important as well because the idea of the welfare state codifies our collective obligations toward one another and defines the terms of membership in the national community. By tightening the links between benefits and employment, the late-twentieth-century welfare state has stratified Americans into first- and second-class citizens and undermined the effective practice of democracy. Everywhere market price has superseded social justice.

. . . .

The word *welfare* initially meant "well-being." In the U.S. Constitution, the promotion of the "general welfare" referred to government's advancement of the well-being of the entire population. Early-twentieth-century references to "welfare" in social policy usually meant "child welfare"—the provision of services to orphaned, neglected, and abandoned children. In the second decade, county superintendents of the poor proudly renamed themselves public welfare officials, and state governments replaced boards of state charities with departments of public welfare that centralized and modernized the administration of welfare. In those years, *welfare* rang with a progressive tone; it signified the increased assumption of public responsibility for dependence, the professional administration of programs, the rejection of charity, and the initial steps of the recognition of entitlement.[1]

Thus, in his second biennial report, the Pennsylvania Secretary of Welfare proudly observed that his department, created in 1921, "embodied the most advanced social policy in state administration in the field of charities and correction." When New York City reorganized its Department of Public Charities in 1920, it chose to call it the Department of Public Welfare to express its "broader purpose" and the rejection of outmoded ideas of philanthropy. In 1923, the *Annals of the American Academy of Political and Social Science* devoted a special issue to public welfare. In his foreword, *Annals* editor Clyde King remarked on the recent emergence of public welfare as a modern replacement for outmoded methods of relief. "A decade ago," he wrote, "the Department of Public Welfare was a new ideal just finding official favor in cities and in states" as "the older idea of charities and corrections" retreated before "the newer conception of protection and . . . public welfare."[2]

The early state public welfare departments bundled together a variety of tasks previously performed by several state agencies. For instance, the Massachusetts Public Welfare Department, founded in 1919, oversaw "mental diseases, correction, hospitals and schools, aid and relief." City departments applied the term "public welfare" to an even more diverse set of activities than did either states or counties.[3] The concept of welfare extended beyond the public to the private sector, where it referred to a broad array of activities intended to promote the well-being of workers. These functions included help with buying a home; stock purchase plans; insurance against accident, illness, old age, and death; old-age pensions; medical services; classes and sports programs; land for gardening; improved plant working and safety conditions; and assistance with a variety of personal problems. Together, these activities were known as "welfare work." In the early-twentieth century, welfare work became a national movement as employers experimented with methods designed to reduce labor turnover, boost production, and counteract attempts to unionize their workforces. The National Civic Federation, an employers' organization, even formed its own Welfare Department in 1903, while large corporations appointed "welfare secretaries" to administer their programs and universities began to train students in welfare work.[4]

"Welfare" clearly retained its Progressive Era association with modernity, progress, science, and efficiency and with services rather than relief. In the 1930s, the word *welfare* rarely appeared alone. More frequent were discussions of "social welfare" or "public welfare," terms that stood for a broad array of programs designed to ensure economic security for all. In June 1934, President Franklin Delano Roosevelt appointed the Committee on Economic Security to determine the best way to safeguard Americans "against misfortunes which cannot be wholly eliminated in this man-made world of ours." The committee called for a far-reaching program that included insurance against unemployment, old age, and sickness; expanded public health programs; pensions for the uninsured elderly; and aid for "fatherless children." The Economic Security Act of 1935—the charter of the federal welfare state—embraced the committee's comprehensive understanding of welfare, which encompassed both public assistance—that is, means-tested relief programs such as Old Age Assistance and Aid to Dependent Children—and social insurance, which included contributory programs whose benefits were not tied to income or assets, such as Old Age Insurance (popularly known as Social Security) and unemployment insurance.[5] With these programs, Roosevelt sought to create a system of economic security that replaced the old poor laws and their invidious distinctions with the entitlements of citizenship.

This broad definition of welfare persisted into the years after World War II. In 1946, a Brookings Institution report described federal welfare responsibilities as "education, health, employment and relief, and social security." In 1947, Congress's definition of "public welfare" included services designed to meet a wide array of needs, from helping families reach self-support to overcoming "problems resulting from parental neglect" and foster care. The positive connotations of "welfare state" were so entrenched that the *Saturday Evening Post*'s editors advised critics to avoid the term when discussing President Truman's plans to extend social benefits. "The opponents of such a system," they wrote, "have an excellent case, but they do not help it by adopting precisely the words which put it in a favorable light. 'Welfare' is the key word. Who's against welfare: Nobody. . . . Fighting an election by opposing welfare is on a par with taunting an opponent for having been born in a log cabin."[6]

And yet within a decade, *welfare* had lost this inclusive and positive meaning. The American public welfare state had split linguistically along two of the tracks that divided it administratively: public assistance and social insurance.[7] Welfare now signified only public assistance—which to most people meant Aid to Dependent Children—while Social Security, along with other social insurance programs, was no longer viewed as a form of welfare. Welfare was a despised program of last resort primarily for the "undeserving" poor—unmarried mothers, many of them black and Hispanic. The stigmas of race and sex hovered over public assistance; the aura of work and saving surrounded social insurance. Social Security, with its articulate middle-class supporters, absorbed the "deserving poor" and remained unassailable. These differences in valuation carried enormous consequences. Social insurance programs often lifted their beneficiaries out of poverty; public assistance almost never did—it just helped them to survive.

The process of bifurcation was gradual and, paradoxically, rooted in optimism. The federal officials who administered America's early social welfare programs promoted social insurance and tried to differentiate it from public assistance. They expected public assistance to "wither away" as more and more Americans became paid-up members of the social insurance system. And they believed that the unitary idea of welfare advocated by the Committee on Economic Security threatened to retard the progress of social insurance by tainting it with the historic stigma of "the dole" carried by public assistance.[8] In addition, between 1939 and 1956, Congress aided the devaluation of public assistance by extending social insurance from just the unemployed and retired workers to more and more groups: widows and dependents, the self-employed; domestic, agricultural, and railroad workers; and the disabled. Public assistance began to appear increasingly residual—a category of aid for those few left over.

Initially, the new insurance system for the elderly proved a hard sell. In 1940, Old Age Assistance, the major form of public assistance at the time, paid benefits to 2.07 million people, while Social Security's elderly beneficiaries numbered only 131,000. Even as late as 1949, Old Age Assistance beneficiaries outnumbered those of Social Security by a third—2.49 to 1.67 million. In 1940, Old Age Assistance paid benefits to almost twice as many persons as ADC, and during World War II, a time of full employment, the number on ADC fell while the number of elderly receiving benefits continued to rise. "Relief" conjured up a destitute old person, not an unmarried mother with children.[9]

Although by 1950, the expectation that social insurance would supplant public assistance did not appear unreasonable, events soon overturned predictions. Within a decade, the belief that public assistance would wither away appeared a quaint notion of the recent past. In 1955, for the first time, more persons received benefits under Aid to Dependent Children than Old Age Assistance. The 1960s proved the catalytic decade for AFDC—as of 1962 the new name for ADC—with an astonishing 169 percent rise. Between 1970 and 1975, while Old Age Assistance plummeted 99 percent and nearly disappeared, AFDC grew another 30 percent.[10]

As one group after another left public assistance for social insurance, those who remained—mainly single mothers with children—inherited the degraded mantle of "outdoor relief." First, hostility to ADC increased in some states when voters learned that families with "several children" often received benefits larger than the average earnings of workers "living in the same communities."[11] As a result, at least one midwestern state lowered its benefits. Then, the relief scandals of the late 1940s and early 1950s furthered the equation of public assistance, women, and immorality. A 1947 headline in the *New York Times* proclaimed, "Woman in Mink with $60,000 Lived on Relief in a Hotel"; the "woman in mink" was an unmarried mother. A 1949 *Saturday Evening Post* piece, "Detroit Cracks Down on Relief Chiselers," used only women or families with children as examples; in 1951 another *Saturday Evening Post* article on Oklahoma, "The Relief Chiselers Are Stealing Us Blind," described only abuses under ADC.[12]

But alleged fraud did not yet equate relief with welfare. Nor did welfare yet conjure a narrowly conceived image of morally suspect women. Instead, welfare became controversial in the 1950s because of its correlation with the welfare state—and through the welfare state with socialism. Welfare fell from its protected shelf as one more victim of the cold war.

American critics associated the welfare state with the regimentation, loss of freedom, and heavy-handed state paternalism they equated with socialism. In New York, Governor Dewey warned an audience, "The self-feeding, ever-growing, nobody-can-feed-you-but-us philosophy of the welfare state is not to be confused with the ever-present motive and power of the free modern state to serve its people." A writer in the *Catholic World* argued, "The support of something called welfare now has led to a far more formidable institution, namely the Welfare State, which provides not merely for aid to the helpless but undertakes to enlist all in a great national economic organization supervised by the State. . . . This is Socialism—British Fabian Socialism." An editorial writer in the *Saturday Evening Post* admonished, "Nearly forty years ago, Hilaire Belloc called the Welfare State by a more accurate name, 'the Servile State,' judging correctly that the masses under any managed economy would wind up as slaves—petted and pampered slaves, if they were docile, but slaves in the sense that they would own nothing but a license to earn a living, revokable by someone else." In 1950, members of Congress made speeches titled "The Creeping Shadow of Socialism" and "The Case against the Welfare State."[13]

President Truman deplored the campaign to characterize the "welfare state" as un-American and subversive. In Truman's administration welfare retained its broad and general meaning. His 1948 budget report, for instance, referred to the funds set aside for both Old Age Insurance and Unemployment Insurance as "welfare trust funds." In 1949, he warned against "a new set of scare words" deployed by "the selfish interests" who had opposed his proposals for economic security. Earlier, he pointed out, opponents of Franklin Delano Roosevelt and the New Deal had tried to scare voters with terms like "socialism" and "regimentation." But when these failed to arouse the electorate, critics turned to "bureaucracy" and "bankruptcy." "Now," Truman said, smarting from another lost election, "they're talking about 'collectivism,' and 'statism,' and 'the welfare state.' "[14]

Neither Truman's inclusive use of "welfare" nor his refusal to stigmatize the welfare state prevailed. Instead, by the late 1950s, all the pieces needed for a narrow, derogatory definition of welfare had fallen into place. Public policy had cemented a wall between public assistance and social insurance. Social insurance had drained public assistance of most of the sympathetic or "deserving" poor. Scandals had tainted the image of public assistance, increasingly seen as a program for unmarried mothers and their children. And the cold war association of the welfare state with socialism stripped away the favorable meaning that welfare had held for many Americans. "Welfare" now emerged as a term ready for application to programs that aided the "undeserving poor."

Four related trends accelerated the transmutation of welfare into a synonym for AFDC. First, the social work profession underwent a radical transformation from its origins in helping poor people find food, shelter, clothing, medical care, and jobs to an emphasis on practicing psychotherapy, which increased the divide between public assistance and social insurance. As social workers became increasingly professionalized, public assistance offices were staffed largely by untrained workers; in 1950, only one in twenty-five public assistance workers had a professional degree.[15] The split between social work and the administration of AFDC widened the separation of services from relief and, later, "welfare."

The second trend was the ever-tighter equation of AFDC with race. The proportion of black ADC recipients increased sharply during the late 1940s and 1950s. By 1961, it had reached about 40 percent, which is where it more or less has remained. In some places, the number was much larger, reinforcing the association of ADC and race. The third trend was the rising number of out-of-wedlock births to mothers on AFDC. Between 1950 and 1960, the proportion of children on the ADC rolls who were "illegitimate" increased 25 percent, to 34 percent of black and 10.9 percent of white children—both figures much higher than those for the whole population. The explosive increase of the ADC caseload was the fourth trend. Between 1950 and 1970, the number of AFDC recipients grew by 333 percent—not only as a consequence of the rising number of single mothers but also as a result of Supreme Court decisions and the efforts of welfare rights activists that dramatically increased the proportion of eligible women who actually received AFDC.[16]

By the mid-1960s, the idea of "welfare rights" illustrated the unquestioned equation of welfare with AFDC by the political left as well as the right. In 1966, when poor women joined together to advocate for more generous AFDC benefits and more humane administration of politics, they called themselves the National Welfare Rights Organization. The association of "welfare" with "rights" reflected a strategy designed to link welfare with the civil rights movement and break the lingering association of public assistance with charity and poor relief. The strategy found support in an influential article in the *Yale Law Journal* by Charles Reich, who argued that welfare represented one among several forms of "new property" guaranteed by the Constitution. In a series of major decisions, the U.S. Supreme Court supported the idea of welfare as a right by asserting the entitlement of AFDC recipients to due process and other procedural guarantees of fair and equitable treatment from public authorities. As a result, the proportion of eligible recipients who received benefits rose from about a third in the 1960s to 90 percent in 1971. But the Supreme Court could not abolish the stigma attached to welfare, nor did it make welfare a permanent right.[17]

Instead, the narrow and derogatory definition of welfare directed discussions of public policy along separate tracks. With the exception of Medicare, social insurance programs tied benefits to employment. Their association with work—and the benefits they delivered to the middle class—solidified their hold on public support, and they provided the most generous benefits in America's public welfare state. Welfare, or public assistance, traveled a different route. Tied increasingly to people out of work, unmarried mothers, and people of color, welfare exchanged its early favorable connotation for an association with the undeserving poor. The pejorative connotation of welfare was reinforced by the private sector, which, after World War II, replaced the language of welfare work with that of employee benefits, which no one now calls welfare.

The division of welfare and social insurance along separate discursive as well as policy tracks created fictive distinctions between categories of need and set the beneficiaries of public social provision against one another, leaving them politically vulnerable. The restriction of welfare to the nonworking poor left many workers who were struggling to stay self-sufficient hostile to anyone who appeared to get cash and other benefits without working. More broadly, struggles over welfare directed attention away from the falling wages, growing inequality, and erosion of public benefits that threatened everyone except a fortunate minority. Today, the condemnation of welfare continues to inhibit the development of coherent policy. It permits a president to claim that abolishing AFDC and eliminating entitlements to public assistance represent "ending welfare as we know it," when the most extensive and costly parts of American welfare remain scarcely touched. And it justifies a "welfare reform" that heightens the risks and worsens the poverty that welfare was invented to remedy.

1

THE AMERICAN WELFARE STATE

By focusing attention on public assistance, the language of welfare has obscured the true size and scope of America's welfare state. In reality, it is neither public nor private, but an enormous structure that combines the two. A public branch with three divisions—public assistance, social insurance, and taxation—intersects in a myriad of ways with a huge private branch divided between the independent sector—charities and social services—and employee benefits. In the 1970s, fissures began to appear in the edifice of this rickety structure; by the 1980s, the fissures had turned into giant cracks. By the end of the twentieth century, the war on dependence, the devolution of authority, and the application of market models to social policy had infiltrated every one of its corners. To understand how this occurred, we must look back at how the welfare state was constructed and elucidate the forces that shook its foundation.

The Architecture of the American Welfare State

The term "welfare state" refers to a collection of programs designed to assure economic security to all citizens by guaranteeing the fundamental necessities of life: food, shelter, medical care, protection in childhood, and support in old age. In America, the usual restriction of the definition of welfare state to government programs mistakenly excludes the vast array of private activities that address economic security and the needs associated with poverty and dependence. Thus, "state," as in welfare state, means not only the agencies of federal, state, and local government; it includes both government funding of nominally private organizations to carry out public tasks and private activities heavily regulated by public authorities. "State" is a shorthand for a web of government programs and the quasi-public, quasi-private organizations they finance and regulate. Understood this way, a vast and intricate American welfare state emerges.[1]

The American welfare state resembles a massive watch that fails to keep very accurate time. Some of its components are rusty and outmoded; others were poorly designed; some work very well. They were fabricated by different craftsmen who usually did not consult with one another; they interact imperfectly; and at times they work at cross-purposes. Neither a coherent whole nor the result of a master plan, the public and private programs of America's welfare state originated at different times and from different sources; they remain loosely coupled at best. Yet together they are the means by which America delivers security and support to its citizens. This modern welfare state touches everyone. Because few people can afford to pay the full cost of their medical care or retirement, some welfare state benefits—Social Security and Medicare—are universal and reach beyond the poor. Other programs extend into the ranks of the employed, where many people earn wages too low to lift themselves above poverty through work alone. The welfare state nonetheless has boundaries, however imprecise. Indeed, even though the national government provides huge subsidies to business and the wealthy, the concept of the welfare state should not include all government benefits.[2] To embrace all government subsidies would rob the term "welfare state" of its historic focus on economic security, poverty, and dependence.

Welfare is as old as the Colonies and as American as Thanksgiving. Public assistance, the original component of America's welfare state, began with early colonial poor laws adapted from British practice. Variously called outdoor relief and poor relief, sometimes just relief, later general relief, and, as we have seen, after the 1960s, welfare, it has proved inescapable and unavoidable; for centuries, all attempts to do away with it have failed. The stigma attached to public assistance has proved equally enduring; its beneficiaries have consistently composed the "undeserving poor."

Public assistance is marked by two other characteristics. First, it has always been, and remains, administered and funded locally rather than federally, at least in part. Originally, counties and towns operating under loose state laws bore almost exclusive responsibility for poor relief. During the nineteenth century, states increased their involvement and oversight. The federal government, however, ran large public assistance programs for only a few years during the Great Depression. The two federal programs introduced in 1935—Aid to Dependent Children and Old Age Assistance—were administered by the states, which were allowed to set benefit levels, and which drew their funding from their own as well as federal treasuries. As a consequence, benefits varied greatly throughout the nation.

Second, public assistance has always been inexpensive. Governments complain about its cost, but it is a bargain compared to other programs, and its low cost is one key to its staying power. Throughout American history, it is hard to imagine a cheaper means of keeping people alive. Though public assistance has caught most of the hostility to welfare, it forms a very small part of the welfare state. In 1995, the total cost of AFDC was $22 billion, of which the federal government paid $12 billion and the states the rest. AFDC amounted to less than 1 percent of the gross domestic product (GDP). Together, in 1995, the three major federal and federal-state public assistance income support programs—AFDC, food stamps, and Supplemental Security Income—amounted to 4.4 percent of the federal budget. About 14 million individuals, more than 9 million of them children, received support from AFDC, 27 million from food stamps, and 6.5 million, roughly 80 percent of whom were disabled, from SSI. (The number of recipients of the program that replaced AFDC fell dramatically after 1996.)[3]

The cost of social insurance programs dwarfs public assistance. Called "insurance" because they require the payment of "premiums" by individuals or employers, these programs provide uniform benefits to everyone who meets fixed criteria (such as age), regardless of income or assets. Public social insurance began with workers' compensation in the early-twentieth century. By the 1930s, a few states had taken tentative steps toward unemployment and old age insurance as well. With the Economic Security Act of 1935, often referred to as the Social Security Act, the federal government launched social insurance as a series of national programs—the first were Unemployment Insurance and Old Age Insurance. In 1956, Congress added disability insurance, and, in 1965, Medicare.

In the mid-1990s, workers' compensation amounted to about $43 billion a year, twice the cost of Aid to Families with Dependent Children. In 1995, unemployment compensation paid benefits to 7.9 million individuals at a cost of $21.3 billion.[4] Medicare covered about 38 million individuals at a cost of $180 billion, and Social Security benefits reached 43.4 million individuals at a cost of $336 billion, or 21.8 percent of the U.S budget of $1.54 trillion. In 1995, Social Security alone cost five times as much as AFDC, food stamps, and SSI combined. Low to begin with, the real value of AFDC benefits had declined steeply—by 47 percent in constant dollars from 1970 to 1995—while Social Security benefits, which are indexed, kept pace with inflation.[5]

Social Security and Medicare are national programs; benefits do not vary by state. All social insurance programs provide much more generous benefits than do any public assistance programs. "Insurance," however, describes them imperfectly because they are financed not by accumulated contributions but primarily with the payroll taxes of currently employed workers. Because they are universal and share, even if inaccurately, the mantle of insurance, they remain by far the most popular programs in America's public welfare state. And they deserve their esteem: Social Security has cut poverty among the elderly by about two-thirds, while Medicare has vastly improved the access of the elderly to health care.[6]

Social insurance programs, like public assistance, also inscribed race and gender hierarchies into public policy. Social Security and unemployment insurance originally excluded agricultural and domestic workers—in other words, most African Americans and women, who found themselves relegated most often to public assistance, while state governments discriminated against blacks in awarding Aid to Dependent Children. Despite the expansion of "covered" occupations, unemployment insurance continued to discriminate against women and blacks, penalizing them for their customary work histories. And Social Security still tilts away from equitable treatment for married women and widows. Current formulas do not credit the contributions of many previously employed married women toward higher benefits, and they maintain a very large gap between the benefits of couples and of survivors. Nevertheless, Social Security has worked a revolution in the experience of elderly women, who compose the majority of its beneficiaries. African Americans confront the irony that programs that serve them less adequately than whites nevertheless assure many a level of regular support previously unknown and remain the only shield between them and economic disaster.[7]

The public welfare state's use of taxation to promote economic security is much less well known and less appreciated or disliked than either social insurance or public assistance. With good reason, political scientist Christopher Howard calls taxation the "hidden welfare state." The tax code delivers benefits indirectly through incentives and directly through tax credits and deductions. Employers who offer health and retirement benefits are allowed to deduct their expenses from their incomes. (Of course, this benefits all workers, not just those with low incomes.) The tax code is designed to stimulate the construction of low-income housing and jobs by offering developers and businesses tax credits, such as the Low Income Tax Credit, worth $495.5 million in 1994. Tax-based incentives also underlie recent urban policies designed to revive inner cities by attracting businesses and investment. In 2000, Republicans proposed using tax credits to extend health insurance to many of the uninsured. The federal Work Opportunity Tax Credit, the

Welfare to Work Tax Credit, and various other state subsidies and tax credits all encourage employers to hire welfare recipients. In 1993, the cost of "tax breaks for social purposes"—cash equivalents and deductions for pensions and private social benefits—was more than twice the amount spent on AFDC.[8]

The Earned Income Tax Credit is a dramatic example. It delivers benefits directly: individuals receive checks for the amount owed to them by the federal government. As a result of President Bill Clinton's expansion of EITC, in 1996 the federal government predicted that 18 million people would claim the credit, at a cost of $25.1 billion. The EITC, which paid money to more people and at a greater cost than that of AFDC, emerged as the federal government's primary means of boosting the working poor over the poverty line. With virtually no opposition, the Clinton administration engineered a massive increase in an income transfer program at a time when other forms of social welfare faced only real or proposed cutbacks.[9]

The private welfare state is as complicated and varied as the public one. The charity and social services sphere, or "independent sector," encompasses everything from small soup kitchens to the massive Catholic Charities USA, with an annual budget of about $2 billion. It also includes foundations, social services like Meals-on-Wheels and foster care, and organizations devoted to single issues, such as the American Heart Association. Although the independent sector has never met all the needs of poor or otherwise dependent Americans, its essential components—charity, voluntarism, and philanthropy—can claim a long history and an essential role in American social welfare. In the mid-1990s, the best estimate put the independent sector's annual cost at $568 billion (roughly the cost of Social Security and Medicare combined) and the number of its institutions at more than one million.[10]

Employee benefits exceed even those of the independent sector. Most Americans receive their health care and part of their retirement income through this private welfare state. To be sure, benefits contingent on employment and, to some extent, on the goodwill or enlightened self-interest of employers are an imperfect replacement for universal public entitlements. But they amount to significant spending that in other countries often comes from the public treasury. International comparisons of U.S. social spending frequently fail to include private benefits. At 7.82 percent of GDP, America's 1993 "voluntary private social expenditures" far exceeded those of other advanced nations: 3.19 percent in the United Kingdom, 0.97 percent in Sweden, and 1.47 percent in Germany. The importance of the private welfare state cannot be underestimated, not only because of its impact on the security and well-being of Americans, but also because of its cost—in 1992, $824 billion.[11]

American social policy has always carried out public purposes through private agencies. In the early-nineteenth century the state of New York contributed public funds to a private philanthropy for the education of New York City's poor children. Some state governments tried to meet the growing demand for secondary education by chartering and subsidizing private academies. State governments paid private orphanages to care for needy children and hospitals to treat the sick. They granted private agencies—the Society for the Prevention of Cruelty to Children, for instance—police powers to intervene in cases of suspected child abuse and neglect. American government, in Alan Wolfe's trenchant phrase, has always operated partly as a "franchise state." It is the way the nation builds missiles and delivers social services; increasingly, it is the way it punishes convicted criminals. Indeed, in recent years social service agencies and charities have drawn even closer to public authorities as providers for the state. Nor is the private welfare state of employee benefits exempt from government influence: enormously complicated regulations and legislation govern the administration of private pension plans and other benefits, such as health and family leave policies.[12]

America's welfare state not only retains a mixed economy, it also remains remarkably local and decentralized. Recent welfare reform not only preserved the vast variation in benefit levels among states, it encouraged yet more variety by devolving significant authority to state governments, which, in turn, are at liberty to cede much of the administration and rule setting for public assistance to counties. Although Social Security, Medicare, food stamps, and the Earned Income Tax Credit are national programs, two crucial components of social insurance—workers' compensation and unemployment compensation—are partially or wholly state programs that differ widely in eligibility rules and benefits. Medicaid, a key component of the public assistance safety net, is also a joint federal-state program that allows states discretion in setting benefits and reimbursement amounts. Block grants for child welfare are another example of the way the federal government promotes local variation in the welfare state. And, of course, the private welfare state provides benefits and services through literally millions of agencies and employers, which, despite federal and state regulations and the strings attached to grants, retain a great deal of autonomy.

Its links to employment, as well as its decentralization, distinguish the American welfare state from its counterparts in other industrial nations.

For most nonelderly Americans, access to health care depends on having a job with medical benefits, or being a dependent of someone who does. In no other modern industrial nation is health care an earned privilege rather than a human right. Throughout American history, welfare reformers have tried to couple public assistance and private charity with employment by devising work tests to separate the deserving from the undeserving poor. Nineteenth-century Charity Organization Societies sent men who applied for help out to cut wood or break stone. Poorhouses tried, without much success, to put their inmates to work. During years of great industrial upheaval, public officials and the leaders of private philanthropy demonized out-of-work men as lazy tramps. For many years, the opposite was true for working mothers: advocates of mothers' pensions in the years 1910–19 and Aid to Dependent Children in the 1930s hoped public benefits would permit mothers to stay at home with their children, or at least work only part-time. They viewed full-time work among mothers as a source of family pathology, not a means for overcoming it. In recent years, of course, all this has changed. With the passage of "welfare reform" in 1996, the links between employment and public assistance tightened. Welfare reform transmuted survival itself into a privilege contingent on work.[13]

The American welfare state also stands out for what it lacks. America has what I have called a "semi-welfare state"; others have referred to it as incomplete or truncated or have called America a welfare laggard. Whatever the label, the evidence is clear and familiar: America, unlike other advanced nations, lacks national health insurance. It has no family allowance. It permits more of its children to remain in poverty than does any comparable country. It offers unmarried mothers less help with either day-to-day survival or the transition to independence than do most other industrial nations. It provides far fewer of its citizens with publicly supported housing than do European nations, and it restricts what Europeans calls "social housing" to the very poor. It spends far less on active labor market policies, such as job training and job creation. In 1990, among eight advanced countries, only Japan, at 11.2 percent of GDP, ranked lower than the United States at 11.5 percent in public outlays on pensions, health insurance, and other income maintenance. For France, spending amounted to 23.5 percent of GDP and for Germany, 19.3 percent. Although European nations have recently moved in the direction of American practice, the distinction between continents remains unmistakable, at least for the present. With the United States considered as 1, the 1993 ratios of public social spending were:

United Kingdom   1.50
Sweden   2.54
Germany   1.91

However, with private social benefits included, the ratios drop and the United States seems less of an outsider, although it still ranks last compared with advanced European nations.

United Kingdom   1.16
Sweden   1.73
Germany   1.35

Including tax deductions and credits would reduce the disparity even more.[14] Still, the United States remains distinct because it spends less on social programs and because it calibrates the balance between public and private in a different way than European nations do.

The results of public intervention in labor markets highlight other differences between U.S. and European social policy. In the 1980s and 1990s, U.S. unemployment rates remained consistently lower than those in most western European countries. This enviable situation, it was usually argued, resulted from the lighter hand of government and freer markets—specifically, the far less regulated American labor market and a low and falling rate of unionization. In Europe, the theory went, unionization kept wages artificially high and depressed employment, and welfare states that influenced the supply and demand of labor had the perverse effect of increasing unemployment.

Contrary to this conventional story, however, official unemployment rates in the United States appear lower only because they omit inmates of prisons and jails. The United States incarcerates a far higher proportion of its population than does any western European country. The average rate of incarceration in sixteen Organization for Economic Development and Cooperation countries in 1992–93 was 78 per 100,000 population. In the United States it was 519—1,947 for blacks and 306 for whites. This extraordinary U.S. figure bears no relation to differences in violent crime rates. Rather, it reflects changes in criminal justice practices, including tougher sentencing and the criminalization of drug-related activity. By correcting unemployment for incarceration, Bruce Western and Katherine Beckett have shown that the U.S. rate rises by about 2 percentage points. This corrected rate approaches rates in some European countries and exceeds those of others. Factoring in incarceration also raises the rate of joblessness and qualifies the image of economic recovery in the 1990s. About 40 percent of African American men over the age of twenty have been out of the labor force at all times during the last two decades, through prosperous times as well as recessions.

This high rate of incarceration does more than mask real unemployment and joblessness; it contributes to both by reducing the job prospects of ex-convicts. Not surprisingly, they have more difficulty finding work, and they often end up back in prison. This perverse effect of imprisonment proves especially long lasting for youth. It is true that European welfare states reduce labor force participation by making it possible to live without work. But in the process they also redistribute income and increase equality. In Europe, tax and transfer policies lift about half the nonelderly poor out of poverty. In the United States, where the figure is much lower, the dynamic is reversed. There, the impact of incarceration registers most heavily on those with the least power in the labor market—young, unskilled minority men, who are imprisoned at a far higher rate than that of any other group. As a consequence, America's de facto labor market policy, administered through the penal system, heightens poverty and increases inequality.[15]

Still, the frustrating limits that hobble America's welfare state should not obscure its achievements. Compared to the situation at the start of the last century, public programs have dramatically alleviated the consequences of poverty and dependence. In America's cities, millions of women and men who at the start of the twentieth century would have suffered desperate poverty now, at the turn of the next century, live with a sense of security and in modest comfort. Others, although they remain poor, find survival incomparably more assured than they would have a century ago. Without Social Security and Medicare, old people suffered extraordinary poverty and lacked access to adequate health care. Without AFDC or food stamps, single mothers with children could only beg a pittance from the suspicious agents of charity. Without unemployment insurance, workers' compensation, and disability insurance, employees injured on the job or thrown out of work lacked any public source of assistance other than tiny, sporadic amounts of relief, accommodation in a poorhouse, or temporary lodging in a police station or homeless shelter; they found it hard, if not impossible, to locate private charity, which remained uncertain and inadequate. Poverty and dependence in America have never been easy or pleasant to endure, but a century ago they were immeasurably worse.[16]

Welfare and the Conservative Ascendancy

The resurgence of conservatism in late-twentieth-century politics and culture inspired attacks on the huge, imperfectly articulated American welfare state. Building on a demographic base in the South and the sub-urbs, conservatism responded to the anger and confusion of ordinary Americans experiencing economic insecurity and a new racial order. The movement drew strength from its affiliation with evangelical and fundamentalist Protestantism, from ideas disseminated by conservative think tanks underwritten by big money, and from the perceived failures of government and the collapse of communism.[17]

Conservative policy was one among the possible responses to real problems. Its ascendance signaled first of all a victory for international business. In the 1970s, relentless international competition forced busi-nesses to reduce costs by downsizing, restraining wages, attacking unions, reducing benefits, and pressuring governments to cut back on welfare states. The welfare state, they believed, increased the costs of business by raising taxes and forcing business to raise wages to attract workers who found an alternate source of support in public benefits. All over the globe—in Europe, Asia, and Latin America as well as in the United States—the need to control the cost of labor in a global economy ranked high among the influences prompting nations to redefine their welfare states.[18]

National budgets and changing demographics also put pressure on welfare states. The problem was worldwide. In Europe the cost of increased unemployment challenged the fiscal capacity of governments to continue current levels of social spending. Although unemployment was lower in the United States, the situation paralleled Europe's. There, too, a similar contradiction between escalating need and seemingly unsustainable expense overburdened the welfare state, threatening to raise taxes. In addition, a demographic crisis loomed: as the population aged, the number of elderly citizens in need of support grew faster than the number of workers whose taxes supported them. Even though the relative size of the aged population was smaller in the United States than in Europe, its projected cost drove attempts to redesign the welfare state's most expensive programs: Social Security, Medicare, and Medicaid.[19]

In the United States, the cost of both hot and cold war also drew funds away from social programs. Despite his promise of "guns and butter," President Lyndon Johnson's escalation of the Vietnam War in the 1960s undermined the War on Poverty. In the 1970s, the military buildup occa-sioned by competition with the Soviet Union drained funds that might have been spent on domestic programs. In the 1980s, the Reagan admin-istration's "Star Wars" initiative and its massive military spending again diverted limited federal funds away from the welfare state.

In the same years, the economic stress felt by ordinary workers fueled a hostility toward welfare and the dependent poor, driving politics in a conservative direction. Resentments welling up among traditionally Democratic voters led many of them to support George Wallace and, later, Ronald Reagan. As income inequality widened after the early 1970s, workers found themselves running harder just to stay even. With their real wages falling, families needed multiple jobs and income from both husbands and wives. Hundreds of thousands found themselves laid off as a result of downsizing and restructuring. They watched as jobs migrated to Asia, Mexico, or anywhere wages remained lower, and they resented government "handouts" that seemed to reward nonwork and loose morals. Women forced by economic necessity to work, even when they had young children, could not understand why their taxes went to support women who stayed at home.[20]

Desegregation and affirmative action added race to the brew of resentments. In many places, whites objected when court-ordered busing brought black children to their neighborhood schools or forced their own children to travel to distant schools. They watched angrily when federal and local governments used civil rights laws, housing subsidies, and public assistance to support blacks who wanted to move into their neighborhoods. They identified welfare, public housing, and housing subsidies with minorities and wondered at the justice of these benefits when they worked so hard to pay their own mortgages, rent, and grocery bills. White workers thought themselves disadvantaged because, they believed, less qualified blacks were hired or promoted in their place. Government programs associated with liberals or Democrats became the villains, and blue-collar workers moved decisively to the right, where conservative politicians played on their fears. Instead of directing anger at the wealthy and powerful, the fusion of race and taxes deflected the hostility of hard-pressed lower- and middle-class Americans away from the source of their deteriorating economic position and toward disadvantaged minorities—and, in the process, eroded support for the welfare state. This working-class move to the right did not confine itself to the United States, as the popularity of Margaret Thatcher in Britain and the rise of right-wing populist political movements in continental Europe reveal. There, too, racial animus, directed mainly toward immigrant workers and their families, joined economic insecurity to propel politics rightward and weaken popular support for welfare states.[21]

The increasing prominence of the Sunbelt in electoral politics strengthened conservatism's influence. Southern and western conservatism arose not only from lower- and middle-class whites angry at competition from blacks, scared by economic insecurity, and upset at the transformation of the old racial order. It also received strong support, and leadership, from business interests alienated by Democratic economic and natural resource policies.[22] Middle-class suburbanization in the Sunbelt—indeed, throughout the nation—also fueled the new conservative politics. Many suburbanites were the children of white Catholic immigrants, who were angry at busing, threatened by affirmative action, and offended by the behaviors they associated with African American newcomers to their cities. "Suburbia," reported political commentator Kevin Phillips, "did not take kindly to rent subsidies, school balance schemes, growing Negro migration or rising welfare costs. . . . The great majority of middle-class suburbanites opposed racial or welfare innovations." Together, the Sunbelt and the suburbs provided the demographic and political base for the new conservatism, assured the rightward drift of politics among both Republicans and Democrats, and reinforced hostility to public social programs that served the poor—especially where those poor were thought to be mainly black or Hispanic.

As the writing on the political wall became clearer, Democrats, eager to win back business support, "acquiesced in, and in many cases helped promulgate, the right turn in public policy," as Thomas Ferguson and Joel Rogers put it in *Right Turn*. By the 1990s, no administration that wanted to remain in office could propose higher taxes for social spending,[23] and with the New Democrats led by President Bill Clinton, the campaign to redefine the welfare state had become truly bipartisan.

The politics of evangelical Protestants intensified the movement to redefine the welfare state. In the 1970s, appalled at government support for what they considered rampant immorality and threats to funding for Christian schools, they entered politics. With remarkable speed, they built an infrastructure of grass-roots organizations and media outlets. Although they focused on social and moral issues, they made common cause with free-market conservatives and became a powerful force in the movement of American politics to the right and in the attack on the welfare state.[24]

Historically, evangelicals had for the most part stayed out of politics. Before the early 1970s, conservative Christians (a term that includes evangelicals and fundamentalists) distrusted politics, and studies showed even an inverse relation between religious conservatism and involvement in political activities. All this reversed in the 1970s, when conservative Christians entered politics largely to protect families. Only through politics, they came to believe, could they guard their interests and reverse the moral corruption of the nation. Welfare, they thought, weakened the institution of family by encouraging out-of-wedlock births, rewarding sex outside of marriage, and allowing men to escape the responsibilities of fatherhood.[25] Although the Christian right drew its real inspiration from social and moral issues—abortion, school prayer, the teaching of evolution, gay civil rights, and the Equal Rights Amendment—it also forged links with free-market conservatives and conservative opponents of the Soviet Union. Indeed, militant anticommunism fused the strands of the conservative movement around opposition to a common enemy.[26]

Fiscal conservatives won the support of middle-class fundamentalists, first, by linking social programs to moral issues and, second, by appealing to conservative Christians whose "economic fortunes depend more on keeping tax rates low by reducing government spending than on the social welfare programs that poorer fundamentalists might desire," argued Robert Wuthnow and Matthew P. Lawson. The result was a fundamentalist politics opposed to the social and moral tendencies of modern government "but in support of economic policies favorable to the middle-class"—a movement crucial for building both the electoral and financial base of conservatism.[27]

Evangelicals and fundamentalists constitute a powerful political force: in the South, they make up about a third of the white electorate; in the North, a little more than a tenth. In 1980, a leading evangelical strategist, Paul Weyrich, urged evangelical ministers to mobilize their congregations to vote for Republican candidates, especially Ronald Reagan, who had asked evangelicals to help win him the presidency that year. With the support of evangelicals, the New Right won stunning electoral victories throughout the country. By the 1990s, evangelicals and fundamentalists constituted the largest and most influential grass-roots movement in American politics.[28] Its great breakthrough came with the 1994 congressional elections, when, for the first time, a majority of evangelicals identified themselves as Republicans and only one-third claimed to be Democrats. The Christian right, according to one estimate, mobilized 4 million activists and reached 50 million voters. The outcome of the election proved the success of its organizing: the Christian right supported candidates in at least 120 contests for the House of Representatives, and its candidates won 55 percent of them.[29] They were a crucial element in the Congress that voted to "end welfare as we know it."

Political and social movements need money as well as passion. The cash to pay for the rightward movement of American politics and culture and bankroll the attack on the welfare state derived primarily from two sources. Through political action committees the militant right marshaled money for use in elections, referenda, and lobbying, and through the support of nonprofit research centers—"think tanks"—it gathered funds for the production and dissemination of ideas. With funding from conservative foundations and corporations, older institutes reorganized, while newer ones formed to challenge liberalism. The American Enterprise Institute, founded in 1943, reorganized in 1953; the Hoover Institution, started in 1919, severed formal ties with Stanford University in 1959; the Heritage Foundation, originally supported by Colorado brewer Joseph Coors, opened in 1973; and the libertarian Cato Institute opened in 1977.[30]

Within a year of its founding, the Heritage Foundation received funds from eighty-seven corporations and large contributions from six or seven major foundations. Along with other conservative think tanks—notably the Hudson Institute, the American Enterprise Institute, the Adolph Coors Foundation, and Empower America—Heritage worked hard to discredit the welfare state. Concentrated funding streams linked conservative foundations, think tanks, and public policy scholars in a tight and powerful network—a web of foundations, fund-raising organizations, direct mail operations, publications, and mass media connections. The same funders nourished the development of conservative policy on a number of related issues: English only, immigration reform, affirmative action, welfare, tort reform, and campus wars over educational and cultural issues. From 1992 to 1994 twelve conservative foundations with assets of $1.1 billion awarded $300 million in grants. The top five conservative groups worked with revenues of $77 million in 1995, compared to $18.6 million for "their eight political equivalents on the left."[31]

Conservative think tanks not only produce ideas—they market them. The Manhattan Institute funded Charles Murray's anti–welfare state polemic, *Losing Ground*, and spent heavily to promote it to the press and public. In the 1970s, metaphors of "science and disinterested research," prominent during the early history of think tanks, gave way to market metaphors. According to historian James Smith, "marketing and promotion" did "more to change the think tanks' definition of their role (and the public's perception of them)" than did anything else. Conservative funders paid "meticulous attention to the entire 'knowledge production process,'" wrote Smith, which they portrayed as a "conveyor belt" stretching from "academic research to marketing and mobilization, from scholars to activists," and they developed "sophisticated and effective media outreach strategies." In 1995 alone, Citizens for a Sound Economy "produced more than 130 policy papers, conducted 50 different advertising campaigns, appeared on 175 radio and television shows, placed 235 op-ed articles, and received coverage in more than 4,000 news articles." In 1989, the Heritage Foundation spent 36 percent of its budget on marketing and 15 percent on fund-raising, including direct mail to 160,000 individual supporters. Liberal organizations did not begin to match the outreach efforts of conservatives, whose ideas, often unchallenged and based on inaccurate data, powerfully shaped public opinion about politics, the economy, and the welfare state.[32]

The right circumvented the liberal politics of most leading social scientists in the United States first by channeling "lavish amounts of support on scholars willing to orient their research" in conservative directions, and second by adopting a "grow-your-own approach." Conservatives funded "law students, student editors, and campus leaders with scholarships, leadership training, and law and economics classes aimed at ensuring that the next generation of academic leaders has an even more conservative cast than the current one."[33]

In their attack on the welfare state, conservative foundations and think tanks drew on a body of ideas articulated with force and clarity. Martin Anderson, a Republican economist and public policy expert who had worked in both the Nixon and Reagan administrations, described Reagan's 1980 election and subsequent events as the political results of an international intellectual movement that had started in the United States in the 1950s and 1960s. Anderson described the movement to Godfrey Hodgson as "an intellectual revolution moving with the power and speed of a glacier"—proof that "ideas do move the world."[34]

The new conservatism wove together three intellectual strands—economic, social, and nationalist. Its economics stressed free markets and minimal government regulation. Its social impulse led toward the restoration of social order and private morals by authoritarian government. Conservatism's nationalist streak favored heavy public spending on the military. It focused on both the enemy without—the Soviet Union and communism—and the enemy within—anything or anyone that facilitated the socialist takeover of America. Incompatibilities, even contradictions, had threatened to keep the strands of conservatism separate, unable to twist together into a powerful and unified force.[35] The history of conservative thought tells the story of how these incompatible strands fused into a powerful intellectual movement.

Conservative thought found acceptance because it resonated with interests, fears, and hopes as varied and contradictory as the strands that composed it. Some of these have been discussed already: the economic strains on ordinary Americans, the anger and fear aroused by the end of the racial order in the South and affirmative action in the North, the needs of international business, the wage pressures felt by American firms, and the resurgent evangelical Protestantism that spread outward from the South. Hodgson points as well to the belief in American exceptionalism—a patriotism violated, conservatives believed, by the political left, which seemed to take pleasure in the denigration of America. He also stresses the odd populism that fed conservative thought: America's troubles had been brought on by elite easterners who disdained the values and interests of ordinary Americans. A true conservatism would return government to the people.[36]

Conservative thought gained strength, too, from the widespread sense that the federal government's massive social programs launched in the 1960s had failed. Aside from higher taxes, more poverty, dying cities, increased crime, and moral rot, what was there to show for the money and effort? The sense that federal social policy had failed was reinforced by a rejection of the Keynesian economic theories that had justified social spending, an antipathy to politics, and a distrust of government, including the large bureaucracies that administered social programs and institutions. The theoretical attack on activist government, led by University of Chicago economist Milton Friedman, brought great sophistication to the cause of the economic conservatives. "By 1980 the climate of economic thinking in the United States," reports Hodgson, "had changed utterly from the orthodoxy of 1965." Keynesian economics, which had sustained the welfare state, appeared dead.[37]

On a more popular level, distrust of government found expression in Charles Murray's enormously influential *Losing Ground* (1984)—sometimes referred to as the Reagan administration's new bible. Murray, who argued for the withdrawal of government from social welfare, assaulted welfare from a market-based, libertarian, antigovernment perspective. Despite massive government social spending since 1965, he contended, both poverty and antisocial behavior—crime and out-of-wedlock births—had increased. Neither could be traced to economic conditions. Rather, they resulted from rational responses to the perverse, short-term economic incentives built into federal welfare policy. His solution lay in changing the incentives by ending welfare.

Unlike Murray, Lawrence Mead, author of *Beyond Entitlement: The Social Obligations of Citizenship* (1986)—the other major conservative book on welfare published during the 1980s—justified big government in conservative terms. His preferred philosophers were Hobbes, Burke, and Tocqueville, not Adam Smith; he focused on society, not the individual; and he worried more about moral order than liberty. Mead advocated enforced social obligations for the poor. The major problem with government social programs, claimed Mead, lay in their permissiveness, not their size. Although he wanted to inject people into the marketplace, not shield them from it, he still stressed the tutelary role of government. "Government is really a mechanism by which people force themselves to serve and obey *each other* in necessary ways." Social order demanded that government "must take over the socializing role."[38]

Popular conservative books and articles exuded confidence that seemingly intractable national problems could be solved with common sense, sound values, and faith in the capacity of ordinary Americans. At a time when unemployment and inflation together produced a new phenome-non—"stagflation"; when the nation reeled from the humiliation inflicted by Iran's seizure of American hostages; when feminism and affirmative action seemed to threaten traditional family values and opportunity structures; and when crime appeared to rule city streets, the optimism of conservative thought proved one of its most potent appeals. Liberals, by contrast, appeared unable to offer a new vision of America's future, a prescription free of complex government, that could rise above a gloomy and incapacitating account of the structural origins of America's inter-connected and intractable problems.

Ronald Reagan's successful 1980 presidential campaign wove together the three strands of conservatism: the social, economic, and nationalist. Ronald Reagan may have used Murray as his bible on welfare reform, but the major welfare legislation of his term in office owed much more to Mead. Reagan's cheerful theoretical eclecticism characterized his administration, and his optimism reflected the upbeat tone of much conservative literature. Reagan attacked the perceived excesses of liber-alism, championed the replacement of the public by the private sector, and responded to the anger at the decline of America's international power and prestige. The collapse of the Soviet Union, which discredited communism, appeared to vindicate both his foreign policy and his dis-trust of the state. It seemed to offer living proof that the ideas champi-oned by conservatives were destined to sweep all others into history's trash. The reality was more complex, as subsequent events revealed. The unrestrained capitalism that invaded the former Soviet bloc showed the dislocation and misery that unbridled markets and the shredding of social safety nets could create. Still, in the United States, not only com-munism and socialism but social democracy and its offspring, the welfare state, seemed anachronisms, vestiges of a discredited and outmoded political philosophy.

The Soviet collapse did not prove an unmixed blessing for conserva-tives, however. Hostility toward the Soviet Union and communism had given conservatism an enemy that intensified commitment to its cause and fused its internal contradictions into a single movement. With the common enemy removed, what else could provide the glue, the focus, and the energy? To some extent, Islam took the place of communism, and Iraq and Iran replaced the Soviet Union. But they were enemies of a lesser order. Republicans lacked a great enemy, the strain of argu-ments over strategy eroded their unity, and the Democratic Party, cap-tured by the New Democrats, adopted many of their key ideas. As a result, the Republican Party began to fracture as the old strain between social and economic conservatives, papered over but never mended, reappeared.[39]

Whatever happens to the Republican Party should not obscure the larger story: the ascendancy of conservative ideas in American politics at the close of the twentieth century. The New Democrats, led by a Southern Baptist president and vice president, advocated smaller government, encouraged the devolution of federal authority to the states, asserted the superiority of markets, and joined the war on dependence. Thirty years earlier, it would have been unthinkable that a Democratic president would sign a bill ending the entitlement of the poorest Americans to public assistance. With great clarity, President Bill Clinton's endorsement of the "welfare reform" legislation of 1996 signaled the erosion of the principles that had guided the Democrats since the New Deal.[40] Republicans may have lost the battles for the presidency in 1992 and 1996, but conservatives had won the war. One consequence was the redefinition of America's welfare state.

Dependence, Devolution, and Markets

In the 1980s public social policy coalesced around three great objectives that began to redefine the American welfare state. The first was the war to end dependence—not only the dependence of young unmarried mothers on welfare, but all forms of dependence on public and private support and on the paternalism of employers. The second was to devolve authority, that is, to transfer power from the federal government to the states, from states to counties, and from the public to the private sector. The third was the application of market models to social policy. Everywhere, the market has triumphed as the template for a redesigned welfare state. None of these forces originated in the 1980s, but in those years they burst through older tendencies in public policy and joined to form a powerful tide. As a result, with only a few exceptions, political arguments about the welfare state now revolve more around details than great principles.

In the brave new market-governed world, dependence—reliance for support on someone else—signifies failure and the receipt of unearned benefits. Dependents clog the working of markets; they interfere with relations between productive, working citizens. The tendency of capitalism, as Harry Braverman argued in his dystopian account of the future of work, is to clear the market of all but active and able citizens.[41] This reaction against dependence has worked its way into every corner of the welfare state.

Historically, dependence has had various meanings: legal, domestic, economic, and behavioral. According to philosopher Nancy Fraser and historian Linda Gordon, current-day discussions of American social policy, however, have narrowed dependence to stand for the reliance of poor unmarried mothers on public assistance. This new idea of dependence and the "cultural panic" that surrounds it have been reinforced by the association of dependence with sickness in medical and psychological literature, the equation of dependence with immaturity, especially among women, and the American Psychiatric Association's 1980 identification of Dependent Personality Disorder.[42]

In the 1980s and 1990s, political debate reflected this heightened and widespread anxiety about dependence. "Dependency at the bottom of society," writes political scientist Lawrence Mead, "not economic equality is the issue of the day." Dependency politics arose out of Americans' preoccupation with the "nonworking underclass" responsible for "the decay of the inner city."[43] Mead accurately identified a note in American politics that grew louder and more shrill in the debates over welfare reform, but, like Fraser and Gordon, he missed the hostility to dependence that also has surfaced in attempts to reengineer employee benefits, health care, and Social Security by forcing individuals to rely on themselves rather than on the unhealthy paternalism of employers, charity, or the state.

The war on dependence coincided with a new emphasis on the devolution of authority. In the 1960s, an earlier assault on centralization had attacked the great educational fortresses that oversaw school systems. This movement toward educational devolution sputtered and nearly died of some of its own excesses. By the late 1980s, however, amid growing dissatisfaction with the performance of urban schools, it gained renewed strength. All over the country, school systems granted authority to individual schools as reformers pressed hard for autonomy, which they sometimes, as in Chicago, won to a stunning degree. As corporations realized the disadvantages of large size and command-and-control management, they also decentralized decision making to local sites and reorganized along more flexible lines.[44]

Across the nation, state governors also championed devolution. Influenced by market models and frustrated at the rising costs of public assistance, they chafed at federal regulations that, they said, violated the constitutional separation of powers and prevented them from reforming welfare. Everywhere, "one size fits all" became one of the harshest criticisms of social policies and programs. In the 1980s the federal government began to acquiesce and transfer to states many of the services it had funded since the 1970s, leaving states to pay for them as they could. The

1996 welfare bill replaced the federal entitlement to public assistance with block grants to the states, which allowed the states great latitude in designing their own welfare rules and benefits. State governments, in turn, devolved varying degrees of authority—in some states a great deal of authority—to counties to plan and implement their own welfare systems. They also increasingly handed the administration of public assistance and prison management to both nonprofit and for-profit private entities.

The growing reliance on market models in public policy, the third great force redefining the welfare state, also encouraged devolution. In markets, points out economics writer Robert Kuttner, prices rise and fall "instantly and change continually, as they adjust to shifting tastes and costs. . . . Markets epitomize decentralized, atomized decision-making." The values associated with markets have never drifted far from the center of American public policy. What marks the post-1980 period is their hegemony—their replacement of alternative templates in both the public and private sectors. In recent years, writes Kuttner in *Everything for Sale*, "enthusiasts of markets have claimed that most human activity can and should be understood as nothing but a series of markets, and that outcomes would be improved if constraints on market behavior were removed. . . . A more complex view of society has given way to the claim that most issues boil down to material incentives, and most social problems are best resolved by constructing or enhancing markets. And, indeed, fewer people today enjoy protections against the uglier face of the market, or social income as a right of citizenship. More aspects of human life are on the auction block. Champions of market society insist that all of this makes us better off."[45]

"The move to the market is beyond doubt a truly global phenomenon," assert Daniel Yergin and Joseph Stanislaw. During most of the twentieth century, they point out, the state remained ascendant, "extending its domain further and further into what had been the territory of the market." The mixed economy that resulted remained "virtually unchallenged" until the early 1970s, when, with stunning speed, a reaction set in. By the 1990s, government was in retreat everywhere as the focus shifted from "market failure" to "government failure," the consequences that occur "when the state becomes too expansive and too ambitious and seeks to be the main player, rather than a referee, in the economy." This "decamping of the state from the commanding heights marks a great divide between the twentieth and twenty-first centuries."[46]

There are many varieties of markets. All of them, however, are systems of exchange guided, for the most part, by a set of underlying assumptions. Markets assume rationality: rational individuals act in ways that serve their self-interest. Their collective and unimpeded interactions, the theory goes, yield the greatest public good. Because markets enhance both individual freedom of choice and the optimal allocation of scarce resources, they are the ultimate source of liberty and prosperity. It follows—the extreme version of market philosophy—that governments should interfere with markets as little as possible; the ideal government policy toward markets is laissez-faire.[47] Although the welfare economics literature offers a much more sophisticated view of markets and the rationale for regulation, this stark and unqualified version permeates discussions of the welfare state in politics and the media.

In the United States the shift from government to market found bipartisan support. President Clinton's 1997 *Economic Report* emphasized the "advantages of markets" and the circumscribed, if still crucial, role of government. "At the center of the U.S. Economy," claims the report, stands the market: "vibrant competition among profit-maximizing firms has enhanced economic efficiency and generated innovation, giving the United States one of the highest standards of living in the world." Markets process information more efficiently than government, which cannot "duplicate and utilize the massive amount of information exchanged and acted upon daily by the millions of participants in the marketplace." At the same time, markets provide incentives unavailable to governments. "In private markets, buyers and sellers directly reap the benefits and bear the costs of their demand and supply decisions." Incentives not only shape the uses of resources, they encourage the development of innovations that increase efficiency and "new products that raise living standards." Governments, therefore, should limit their role in the private economy. "Initiatives to increase our economy's reliance on markets, and to improve the efficiency of regulation through market mechanisms, reflect an awareness of the tremendous benefit that market forces can bring to bear by employing private incentives to achieve social goals."[48] "Social goals" here include the objectives of the welfare state.

Markets exist in an uneasy tension with welfare states. The act of exchange at the center of the market experience means "that no market goods are available without some effort or sacrifice." Nothing, in other words, is free. The idea that an individual should receive unearned benefits contradicts the core assumptions on which markets rest. The recent application of market models to public policy is an attempt to resolve the contradiction between markets and welfare states by linking benefits more closely to employment, reducing dependence, and privatizing services.[49]

Legislators, journalists, public officials, and representatives of the private welfare state all now apply market models to public policy, with varying degrees of rigor. While economists attempt to work out the implications with mathematical exactness, public officials more often rely on superficial versions of market models that turn into little more than vacuous slogans. Everywhere, though, the language of the market dominates public policy. It has met stiffest resistance in public education, although advocates of vouchers and private school choice have moved from the fringe to the respectable center of debate.[50] It has found more success throughout the welfare state.

The language of the welfare state and public policy too often reifies markets. Markets appear as outside history, culture, and social structure—a force of nature ineluctably leading to a single inevitable set of results. This easy reification obscures the variability of markets that results from the nature of commodities and forms of capital, relations of power between participants, cultural restraints that define what may and may not be sold, and the conditions under which exchanges may take place. "The human economy," wrote the economic historian and social theorist Karl Polanyi and his colleagues, remains "embedded and enmeshed in institutions, economic and non-economic. The inclusion of the non-economic is vital. For religion or government may be as important to the structure and functioning of the economy as monetary institutions or the availability of tools and machines themselves that lighten the load." The literature of economic sociology explores the rich complexity of markets—current economic sociologists view "their primary task to be to show that markets do not simply consist of homogeneous spaces where buyers and sellers enter into exchange with one another"—but political discussions of the welfare state and other public policy issues remain by and large content with loose metaphors and abstract assumptions that rationalize the actions of those who hold power.[51]

Narrowly applied, market models naturally favor certain answers to key questions about the welfare state—questions about the preferred source of benefits and services, the mechanisms for assuring quality and controlling costs, the criteria for deciding who receives help, the role of guarantees and safety nets, and the source of the ultimate responsibility for ensuring economic security. According to market logic, benefits should originate with private, rather than public, agencies wherever possible, and competition between providers should be relied on to improve the quality and efficiency of service. When governments must provide benefits, authority should rest with state and local officials, rather than with Congress or federal agencies, while only those who earn benefits should receive them. Demonstrated need, socially useful labor (for example, volunteering or child raising), or even good behavior do not by themselves earn benefits: only work for pay counts. Benefits are rewards, not entitlements; there should be no guarantees. Ultimately, the responsibility for economic security should rest not with charity, employers, or the state, but with autonomous individuals taking charge of their lives.

This unreflective application of market models to the welfare state ignores crucial and uncomfortable questions. Whom do market-based policies really serve? What are the forms of capital and who controls them? Who actually participates in the exchange, and does it create casualties? The turn to managed care in health policy is a particularly clear example of the imbalance of power inherent in market-based policies. Proponents of managed care predicted that the injection of market practices into health care would lower costs and improve quality. However, when health care reorganized into managed care with astonishing speed, consumers howled in protest at the result. What happened was not what economists call "market failure." To the contrary, the results represented market success because the real consumers in this case were not patients, but businesses. More than any other force, the drive of business to lower the cost of employee health benefits drove the managed care revolution. And managed care served its customers well; costs leveled off for a while; the market worked. A health care market controlled by consumers-as-patients would produce a very different outcome. A similar story could be told about public assistance. The women forced to claim public assistance in order to survive exert little if any influence over the design of newly "marketized" welfare policies. The real exchange links politicians and their constituencies. The commodity is votes, and the desired outcome is reduced welfare rolls, regardless of what happens to those rejected for benefits or terminated from assistance.

An unreflective application of market models to the welfare state suffers, first, from a failure to explore where markets are appropriate and where they are not. And it also fails to appreciate the possible markets that might be constructed within the welfare state to lessen asymmetries of power and redefine the buyers and sellers of its commodities.

The application of market models to the welfare state has proceeded with a cheery enthusiasm that has excluded any serious and sustained debate over their strengths and limits.[52] What public policy needs desperately is a thorough exploration of where market models work, and where they misfire; what they can achieve, and where the hurt they inflict outweighs their benefits; where they do indeed enhance freedom, and where they redefine democracy and citizenship in ways that violate America's best traditions.

A reevaluation is urgently needed—not only because of the scope and expense of the welfare state but also because of its weakened capacity to respond constructively to new forms of poverty and inequality. Recent public policy has focused on the size of welfare rolls, not the sources of poverty among single mothers; the need of homeless people for shelter, not the crisis in affordable housing; the cost of medical care, not its capture by the marketplace. Confronted with a new American city embodying the contradictory legacy of public policy, urban capitalism, and racism, the welfare state has staggered, incapacitated by the forces—the war on dependence, the clamor for devolution, and the reliance on market models—driving its recent history.

2

POVERTY AND INEQUALITY
IN THE NEW AMERICAN CITY

There is a new American city. Its features are inscribed in the miles of abandoned factories visible from the window of a train passing through North Philadelphia on its way to New York City and in the blocks of abandoned housing, resembling nothing so much as the aftermath of war. The new American city can be found in the Korean, Mexican, and other immigrant neighborhoods that punctuate a trip across Los Angeles, the minicities anchored by shopping malls where highways intersect, the segregated towers of public housing, the new immigrant sweatshops, and in both the endless suburbs stretching out from central cities and revitalized downtowns with their festival markets, gentrified housing, and international skylines.

It is tempting—but misleading—to think of the new American city as lacking either social or spatial coherence. An urban form unlike any other in history, this city defies representation by a single image or metaphor. Neither the gleaming skylines of office towers nor the stark silhouettes of high-rise public housing projects embody its meaning. Rather, it is their conjunction that defines the new American city. Its logic lies precisely in its contradictions.

The revolutions in economy, demography, and space that have shaped this new American city have also made it a site of great inequality and new forms of poverty. These developments are pregnant with meaning for America's welfare state.

Economies

The economic transformation of the American city—as profound and radical as the industrial revolution of earlier centuries—reconstructed labor markets in ways that heightened the risks that welfare states had been built to reduce. Between the 1890s and the 1920s, the American industrial city flourished in the North and Midwest. As early as the 1930s, however, industries began to leave the cities of the industrial heartland for the South. Although by the 1950s a close observer could have found signs of trouble in older industrial cities, it was in the 1960s, 1970s, and 1980s that cities began to hemorrhage manufacturing jobs. In a national sample, 30 percent of manufacturing plants that had more than one hundred employees in 1969 had closed by 1976. These closings were spread almost equally across the country, but the loss of manufacturing hit older cities hardest. Between 1954 and 1977 Detroit lost about half of its manufacturing jobs; between 1947 and 1982 the number of manufacturing jobs in Chicago plummeted from 668,000 to 277,000. This deindustrialization reflected the spectacular foreign growth of industries such as electronics and automobiles, as well as corporate America's search for lower wage and production costs in the suburbs, the Sunbelt, and Third World countries. As businesses competing in the new global economy shed workers, cut wages, and reduced benefits, millions of formerly secure employees found themselves redundant—flotsam on the tide of industrial restructuring.[1]

Drained of industrial jobs, many small older cities shriveled. Empty factory hulks, downtowns bereft of commerce, boarded-up houses, and open spaces overgrown with weeds marked cities such as Camden, New Jersey; Flint, Michigan; or East St. Louis, Illinois, as casualties of economic transformation. In one incarnation, the new American city serves as a reservation for the minority poor. Like Native American reservations, some older cities even began to look to casinos to rescue their economic futures. Formerly industrial cities that also performed other economic functions—government, banking, commerce, medicine, education, and culture—fared better. Their nonindustrial heritage cushioned them against the full consequences of the loss of manufacturing. With some difficulty, cities such as Chicago, New York, Boston, and San Francisco survived the transition to a new form of urbanism; others, like Philadelphia and Baltimore, teetered uncertainly between revival and decline.[2]

Government policy fueled the redefinition of city economies. In the 1940s and 1950s, for example, New York City began to lose industrial jobs partly as a result of planning decisions that viewed factories and warehouses as "urban blight." Housing development pushed 100 large manufacturing firms (and 330 firms of all sizes) from the city between 1946 and 1954. At the same time, governments also created massive numbers of city jobs. Between 1929 and 1974, government employment grew more than any other category in the national economy. These jobs were concentrated in central cities as state and local governments, often with federal funds, assumed new responsibilities in housing, social services, medical care, and education. New "government centers" and other public buildings sprouted alongside the institutions of commerce and finance. The expansion of "third-sector" institutions (education, medicine, nonprofit agencies), also energized by federal funds, accelerated central city economic transformation.[3]

By themselves, however, government and third-sector growth proved unable to revive most city economies, and in the late 1970s observers wondered if old central cities retained any purpose. With population, manufacturing, services, and entertainment scattered to suburbs and exurbs, did big older cities still have any importance? In 1980, an urban commission appointed by President Jimmy Carter encouraged older cities to accept their senescence and advised against offering them federal life support. "The nation can no longer assume that cities will perform the full range of their traditional functions for the larger society. They are no longer the most desirable settings for living, working, or producing."[4]

Like other observers, the commission underestimated cities' capacity for redefinition. A new generation of urban economists argued that cities remained important because they concentrated the people and services essential to commerce and finance, and they asserted that suburban well-being depended on the health of central cities. America, they contended, had become a nation of metropolitan *regions,* anchored by central cities. "Regional economies, with cities at the heart, are now the primary engines of our national prosperity," claimed the U.S. Department of Housing and Urban Development.[5]

Indeed, with the economic recovery of the mid-1990s, cities began to experience modest economic improvement. The central city's share of the growth of retail and service jobs increased, while unemployment and poverty rates declined.[6] This modest revival, however, did not reverse the underlying trends that had reconfigured urban economies, leaving them fragile and vulnerable with a great many residents underemployed and poor.

This contradictory aspect of American cities—the coexistence of downtown redevelopment and gentrification with extreme poverty and deterioration—has grown out of their roles as lead actors in the new world economy. In the 1950s international trade consisted primarily of raw materials and resource-based manufacturing. By the 1980s the capital and services industries began to dominate a redefined international economic order, and major cities became, urbanist Saskia Sassen claims, its "command points." Other cities serve the same purpose on a smaller scale. Not just centers of control, cities are also production sites and markets for the "advanced corporate services" that underpin the new international economy: investment, banking, accounting, management consulting, law, and advertising. Cities may not manufacture as many goods as earlier in their histories, but their financial products and services still fuel world trade.[7]

As these new forms of production replace manufacturing, office towers have become the urban factories of the twenty-first century. But they do not provide the opportunity or the security that industrial factories once did. Service jobs are often nonunionized and do not offer the same pay or benefits as the manufacturing jobs they replaced. Moreover, cities, though integrated into the world economy, have also developed local informal economies—activities that generate income "outside the framework of public regulation." This definition, which excludes crime, includes a range of activities from work out of the home to gypsy cabs. In New York City, for example, informal work is found in apparel, accessories, construction, special trade contracting, footwear, toys, sporting goods, furniture and woodwork, electronic components, packaging, and transportation. Grim sweatshops have also reappeared. "From Philadelphia's Chinatown to New York City's Garment District, workers paint a bleak portrait of the industry as a place where earning less than the federally mandated minimum wage is common, overtime pay is rare, and there is no guarantee of a paycheck at the end of a long week of sewing."[8]

Poorly paid, low-skilled work in services and manufacturing is not an occupational atavism. It is crucial to the economies and social structures of modern cities. Indeed, low-wage employment has expanded as a result of recent economic growth. The key to understanding what at first seems paradoxical—the expansion of low-tech work in a modern international city—lies in distinguishing the characteristics of jobs from the industries in which they are found. In other words, the most dynamic, technologically sophisticated industries all include jobs that pay poorly, lack benefits, and lead nowhere. Stock clerks, maintenance workers, and office cleaners work in advanced industries along with actuaries, lawyers, and engineers.

In the new American city the office tower embodies the same economic processes as the sweatshop. Finance, insurance, and other corporate services, as well as retail trade—all growing sectors—pay less money, employ more part-time and female workers, usually lack unions, and show greater income inequality than did the old manufacturing industries. In myriad ways, they encourage informal work. The substitution of services for manufacturing has thus eroded the private welfare state, thereby magnifying the effects of reductions in public benefits.

The manufacturing that remains in cities has not been immune to the forces reshaping labor markets either. In the late 1970s and the 1980s, as manufacturing employers tried to lower costs by organizing production more flexibly, they too began to rely on involuntary part-time and temporary work and outsourcing, which allowed them to lower wages and benefits. These actions—like the expansion of the service sector—hastened the decline of unions and enlarged the informal economy. The spread of informal work detaches more and more people from the protections associated with steady jobs—health, unemployment, and disability insurance; workers' compensation; and pensions—at the very time when the welfare state has restricted access to public assistance and social insurance.[9]

The social and labor structures of the American city have thus split into two vastly unequal but intimately linked economies—intimately linked because only the informal sector can supply the trappings of prosperity that make urban life attractive to the affluent. Affluent urban workers have created lifestyles that depend on a large pool of low-wage workers. They demand personal services, specialty shops, food individually prepared rather than mass-produced, custom-crafted goods, expensive restaurants, and household help. They want doormen for their condos, cleaning services for their apartments, parking attendants for their cars, and delivery boys for their groceries. And their numbers ensure a viable market for these shops and services. The result, David Cay Johnston observes, is a new "servant class." Like corporations, affluent urbanites have outsourced their domestic tasks for much the same reasons of economy and flexibility and with much the same results. The people they hire often work for poverty wages and suffer full exposure to the risks that, in the formal economy, are covered by employers and the state.[10]

Even the explosive growth of services, local retailing, and small-scale manufacturing cannot supply work for all the low-skilled women and men who want it. In Harlem, two researchers discovered, fourteen people apply for every opening in fast-food restaurants. Cities are full of the unemployed, the underemployed, and the marginally employed working for poverty wages, receiving few benefits, vulnerable to the moods of the economy, and hopeless about the future. Economic recovery began to improve circumstances slightly in 1997 and 1998 as unemployment fell. But central city unemployment is still high, and the underlying conditions that make many central city residents vulnerable remain in place—threatening to reverse modest progress during an economic downturn.[11]

In the past, most unemployment among healthy, working-age adults reflected periodic downturns in the economy, seasonal layoffs, or other temporary factors. Now superimposed on these conventional sources of unemployment is a new phenomenon: relatively permanent isolation from the regular labor force, or chronic joblessness. Very large numbers of people have not worked for a very long time, at least in the regular economy; they may in fact never work there, and their life prospects grow ever dimmer. This is another aspect of inequality in the new American city.

Joblessness—whether the product of economic transformation, as William Julius Wilson contends, or the result of individual willfulness, as Lawrence Mead asserts—underlies the concentration of poverty in inner cities and the emergence of an "underclass." Since the 1960s the share of the chronically jobless among the poor and among African Americans has increased steeply. By 1990, 43 percent of adult men and 56 percent of adult women living in high-poverty census tracts were jobless. The tight labor markets of the late 1990s improved prospects unevenly across groups. In May 1998, for example, the unemployment rate among minority youths in central cities remained five times the average unemployment rate for their white peers. In American cities, there is a connection between race, poverty, and chronic joblessness new in the nation's history.[12]

The distance between the regularly employed and the marginally employed; the young lawyer in his condo and the young man who delivers his pizza; or the stockbroker in her office and the woman who empties her wastebasket exemplify the inequalities inherent in the social structure of the new American city. These examples are extreme, but they represent the income inequality that has increased since the early 1970s.[13]

The disassociation of productivity growth from wages also fueled income inequality. For the first time in American history, productivity gains did not translate into rising real wages. Instead, productivity rewarded shareholders and senior management while workers' pay stagnated. This income inequality contributed to the growth of poverty. Between 1979 and 1992, the official poverty rate grew 23.9 percent. Even including inflation and all noncash benefits, such as health insurance, reduces the increase to only 23.6 percent. As a result, in 1992, 14.5 percent of the population, or 36.8 million people, were poor. Even though the economic expansion after 1993 reduced poverty to 12.7 percent in 1998, the rate was still higher than it had been at the end of the last economic expansion in 1969. "For the first time in recent history," two experts on poverty trends wrote in 1995, "a generation of children has a higher poverty rate than the preceding generation, and a generation of adults has experienced only a modest increase in its standard of living."[14]

Not surprisingly, poverty affects children and minorities disproportionately. The rates are staggering. In 1996, 28.4 percent of all blacks and 31 percent of blacks living in central cities were poor. The outlook for children under eighteen was even bleaker. In 1996, more than one in five

(20.5 percent) was poor—up from 16.4 percent in 1979. And with cuts in public assistance, the severity of child poverty worsened. During the economic expansion between 1995 and 1998, the "child poverty gap"— the total amount of money by which the incomes of all poor children fell below the poverty line—declined only 2 percent while the amount that the average poor child fell below the poverty line rose from $1,471 to $1,604. Among blacks the child poverty rate was 39.9 percent and among Hispanics, 40.3 percent. Overall, the young-child poverty rate in central cities was 36 percent, compared to 16 percent in suburbs. Among states the figure varied greatly, from under 12 percent in New Hampshire and Vermont to 40 percent or more in Louisiana and West Virginia. As a group, American children were worse off economically than children in fifteen of eighteen Western industrialized nations.[15]

Economists do not agree on the reasons for the growth in inequality and poverty, and it is clear that no single factor can account for the trends. The culprit is not government social welfare spending, as Charles Murray and other conservatives argue; nor is it the size of the baby-boom generation, the business cycle, or even declining skills. Instead, beneath the increasing inequality and poverty lie profound changes in the structure of the American economy. The transition from manufacturing to services, the shift from permanent, full-time employment to temporary and part-time work, and the growth of chronic joblessness have all helped to create a class of vulnerable Americans who cannot find economic security in work. For these people, the public safety net has gained more importance, even as it frays beneath them.

Demography

Demographic transformation also played a dramatic role in the emergence of the new American city. The modern story begins with the first Great Migration of African Americans to the North. For impoverished southern blacks, northern and midwestern cities beckoned as "lands of hope," and from World War I to 1920, between 700,000 and 1 million blacks moved north while another 800,000 made the journey during the 1920s. The enormous labor demands of the war opened industrial jobs, and reductions in immigration—first by war, later by acts of Congress— created new opportunities as well. Most black migrants went to cities, men at first to the industrial Midwest, women in greater numbers to older cities in the East, where they worked as domestic servants. As a result, black ghettos emerged and expanded in cities across the nation.[16]

The first Great Migration paled in size before the second. Between 1940 and 1970, 5 million more African Americans left the South, mainly for northern cities. They left for several reasons. The results of the Agricultural Adjustment Act (1933) pushed sharecroppers off their land, and the mechanization of cotton harvesting in southern agriculture after the 1940s made their labor increasingly redundant. In fact, the demand for unskilled labor in the Mississippi Delta plummeted 72 percent between 1949 and 1952. Blacks found economic opportunities more abundant in the North, even though they were relegated to the worst jobs; they welcomed escape from southern violence, the relative availability of public services, and access to the ordinary rights of citizens.[17]

The second Great Migration reshaped the demography of cities across the country. Between 1940 and 1970 the size of San Francisco's black population grew from 4,846 to 96,078 and Chicago's from 277,731 to 1,102,620. In 1940, fewer than one in ten Chicago residents were African American—compared to about four in ten in 1980. As a consequence, the relatively small ghettos of the first Great Migration expanded, intensifying residential segregation. The second Great Migration ended in the 1970s, when blacks followed whites in leaving central cities, moving west, even back to the South, and in modest but increasing numbers to the suburbs.[18]

As blacks moved into cities, whites moved out. Between 1950 and 1970, 7 million white people left central cities. Urban housing shortages, inexpensive suburban housing, cheap government-backed mortgages, and the interstate highway system all conspired to lure families out of cities. As a result, the African American share of central city populations increased dramatically. Washington, D.C., became the first majority-black city in the nation, and Detroit and Newark shifted from mostly white to predominantly black in one generation. In northern cities, which became increasingly poor as well as black, the consequences of the Great Migration tightened the association of welfare with race.[19]

Even the number of African American newcomers did not equal the number of departing whites, and central-city populations stagnated or declined in the North and Midwest. Between 1957 and 1990, the population of Rustbelt cities dropped from 25 to 20 million. The size of Sunbelt cities, in sharp contrast, jumped from 8.5 to 23 million—a result largely of the annexation of suburbs as well as of migration. And everywhere, suburban growth outstripped the growth of central cities. Between 1950 and 1970, American cities grew by 10 million people overall, while the suburbs increased by 85 million. In Los Angeles and Houston, the outer rings grew more than three times as fast as the core. Consequently, many older cities experienced serious depopulation—from 1950 to 1980, for instance, St. Louis lost 47 percent of its residents and Detroit lost 35 percent. Of the thirty largest American cities, only eleven contained more residents in 1998 than in 1970. The depopulation of old cities reduced their density and returned stretches of urban space to nature as untended fields of weeds grew up around the abandoned buildings where housing, retailing, or industry once had stood. The brilliant photographer José Camilo Vergara has labeled this landscape the "green ghetto." Complementing this is Vergara's "institutional ghetto," an area where the institutions of criminal justice and public assistance are concentrated, emphasizing their affiliation with race, social control, and the undeserving poor.[20]

Vergara also described a new "immigrant ghetto." The Hart-Celler Act of 1965 eliminated the discriminatory quotas dating from the 1920s and repealed the barriers to Asian entry that originated in the 1880s. The 13,615,895 people who entered the United States legally between 1961 and 1989 were second in number for a thirty-year period only to the immigrants in 1891–1920. The 1980s saw the most immigration, about 6 million people. In fact, if return migration is taken into account, the 1980s was the decade of greatest net immigration in American history. Undocumented or illegal immigrants lift the real number in the 1980s much higher—by 2 to 3 million, according to Census Bureau estimates. This resurgent immigration built new ghettos and redefined the ethnic makeup of many cities. In some cities immigration stanched, and even reversed, population loss, increased the supply of low-wage labor, and fostered new businesses and services. It also put new pressures on local welfare states.[21]

Immigrants not only arrived in greater numbers; they came from different parts of the world as well. In 1900, 90 percent of immigrants arrived from Europe; in the 1980s, only 11 percent originated there. Latin Americans and Asians composed the majority of the new immigrants after 1970, with Asian immigrants making up nearly half by the early 1980s. Among Latin American countries, Mexico contributed the most immigrants. Nonetheless, the total number of nations sending immigrants increased, and the result was the largest variety of arriving nationalities in American history.[22]

Like their predecessors, the great majority of immigrants—in the 1980s about four of every five—settled in metropolitan areas, most in central cities. In America's largest cities immigrants, their children, and African Americans formed a majority of the population. Immigrants did not distribute themselves evenly among the nation's urban areas, however; rather, they clustered in "gateway cities": Los Angeles, Miami/Dade County, New York City, and San Francisco. In 1990, the county with the greatest proportion of foreign-born residents, 45 percent, was Dade County, Florida; immigrants made up 60 percent of Miami's population. Immigrants from Vietnam, Cambodia, and Laos chose to settle in California; Los Angeles, already the world's second largest Mexican city, became the main destination of Koreans. By the 1980s, more than two-thirds of new immigrants entered through the South and the West, and with the exception of New York City, the Sunbelt contains all the gateway cities into which new immigrants poured after 1965. Los Angeles International Airport was the Ellis Island of the late-twentieth century.[23]

The new immigrants probably were a net economic gain for the nation. Their taxes flowed into the federal treasury; their work effort increased productivity; their youthfulness offset the expense of an aging population. They took jobs that no one else wanted. But they also strained the economies of the cities in which they clustered. Their children overcrowded schools. Usually lacking health insurance, they taxed the resources of local emergency rooms and hospitals. When they were out of work or homeless, they claimed help from state and local authorities, while their income taxes and social insurance contributions went mainly to the federal government. State and local governments, in other words, paid most of the bills; the federal government collected most of the money. Not all groups of immigrants did equally well, either. Among Hispanics, poverty rates and other indicators of economic hardship increased alarmingly. The local economic pressure from the new immigrants intensified latent anti-immigrant feelings, now reinforced by the newcomers' cultural differences and dark skins. In the welfare state, anti-immigrant sentiment was written into law in the 1996 welfare bill, which stripped even legal immigrants of the right to many social benefits—an action that was modified, but far from completely reversed, by a later Congress.[24]

The transformation of urban family structure, as well as urban ethnicity, also helped shape the new American city. Women began delaying marriage and childbearing, fewer married at all, and many more worked outside their homes. Only 26 percent of households now consist of married couples with children. Small households organized around work and consumption sustain revitalized entertainment and shopping districts. These concentrations of well-educated women and men with disposable income and few family responsibilities have fueled the multiplication of private cultural/commercial institutions—the coffee bars and superbookstores that help to define the transformed downtowns of American cities, which have become singularly unwelcoming to the homeless and beggars, and singularly unaffordable by any except the affluent.[25]

New family arrangements have also helped to define inner-city neighborhoods. Increasing numbers of white and Hispanic children, and most

African American children, are born out of wedlock. In 1960, single mothers headed about 8 percent of families with children; by 1990, the proportion had increased to nearly 25 percent. Demographers project that one of every two American children born after 1990 will live for some time in a family headed by a single mother. The increase in single-parent families both increased public assistance rolls and instigated the backlash against them: the object of welfare critics became out-of-wedlock births rather than the poverty of poor young mothers.

In 1960, single mothers were often divorced or separated, and many were widows; now, although a majority are still divorced, nearly 40 percent have never married. The proportion varies by race and ethnicity: 21 percent for whites, 56 percent for blacks, and 37 percent for Hispanics. These trends are most dramatic in impoverished areas of cities. In extreme poverty zones, 73 percent of African American families are headed by single women with children. Nonetheless, even in the extreme poverty tracts of central cities only one-third of families received public assistance in 1990. The rise in the minimum wage, the strong economy, and the tight labor market improved the situation somewhat during the 1990s: the median income of black single mothers increased 21 percent, from $12,765 to $15,530 in inflation-adjusted dollars between 1993 and 1996. Still, in 1995, the poverty line for a family of three was a little over $13,000, which means that these increased wages, welcome as they were, did not lift most families far from official poverty.[26]

Poor African American children often die young in American cities. Infant mortality, although it has declined to record lows for the United States, remains unacceptably high among African Americans—twice the level among whites. In several large cities, the African American figure rivals or exceeds the rate in some Third World countries. Nor do the dangers end with infancy. In Harlem, a fifteen-year-old boy has less chance of reaching the age of forty-five than his white peer has of living to sixty-five. In the late-twentieth century, black men in Harlem were less likely to reach age sixty-five than were men in Bangladesh. "Daily life in the inner city can be harrowing," commented *New York Times* columnist Bob Herbert. "Residents are beset with the uncertainty and anxiety that accompany their efforts to cope with poverty, unsafe neighborhoods and persistent racism. . . . Those kinds of stresses evolve in complicated ways into diseases that are killing people." Drug- and gang-related murders are also a source of early death. Between the periods 1957–60 and 1988–90 in Philadelphia, which sadly is not unusual in this respect, the average homicide victimization rate for nonwhite boys soared from 42.6 to 153.0 per 100,000. Among white boys it rose from 2.6 to 33.5. It is much lower for girls. Although urban crime decreased in the 1990s—in some places dramatically—crime rates remain above their levels of thirty years ago. For poor black children the American city is a dangerous place.[27]

Space

The new urban economy and demography occupy transformed space. Architecture critic Michael Sorkin describes it as "a wholly new kind of city, a city without a place attached to it"—an "ageographical city" projected across the nation. "Globalized capital, electronic means of production, and uniform mass culture," he writes, "abhor the intimate, undisciplined differentiation of traditional cities."[28] But they coexist easily with suburbs. Although there are real differences between cities and suburbs, the distinctions between them are shrinking. Cities and suburbs are joined inescapably as different faces of the new American city. More than they realize, suburbanites are clients of the welfare state, and its redefinition hits them as hard, if in different ways, as it does residents of inner cities.

Suburbanization enjoyed its greatest growth after World War II, but its roots stretch far back in American history, when transportation, affluence, and land development began to transform older cities. The Census Bureau gave suburbs official recognition in 1910. Then, for the first time, in the 1920s the suburbs grew faster than cities. By 1950, the suburban population was increasing ten times faster than urban populations. Housing developments, industrial and business parks, shopping malls, and even entertainment complexes now cluster in "minicities" or "edge cities," an urban form unlike any other in history.

Several influences joined to stimulate the exodus from cities. However, in the early stages, the desire to escape blacks generally was not one of them. Rather, with a national housing shortage and cities densely packed, suburbs held a great attraction for young families seeking homes they could own and open space for their children. The federal government helped by underwriting cheap, long-term mortgages with low down payments in the suburbs and refusing to underwrite them in central cities or in desegregated or black neighborhoods. It also hastened suburban growth with federal highway subsidies and the development of the interstate highway system. In the same years, technology facilitated suburbanization as builders learned to mass-produce houses inexpensively and developed mass marketing techniques to sell them.[29]

The benefits of suburban homeownership included more than security and lifestyle. By accumulating equity in their homes, the white suburban middle class built assets. Most blacks, excluded from suburbs and the mortgage market, were unable to replicate white success. Without home equity, they were massively outstripped by whites in capital accumulation. As a consequence, they found themselves far more vulnerable to the common risks of life and far closer to the edge of dependence, with public assistance rather than a home equity loan their likely safety net in times of unemployment.

As industries as well as families left cities, suburbs became the centers of American manufacturing. By 1977, two-thirds of the manufacturing industry in the Philadelphia area was located in the suburbs; in San Francisco, more than 75 percent of the industry; and in Denver, over half. In Chicago, manufacturing employment dropped nearly 50 percent, while manufacturing jobs in the city's outlying region nearly doubled from 278,000 to 521,000. Giant industrial districts surround Los Angeles, while the nation's second largest manufacturing region lies within a sixty-mile radius of New York City.

Retailing and services soon followed the movement of population and manufacturing. Between 1977 and 1982, suburban service jobs grew four times faster than service work in central cities, and by 1988, 59 percent of the nation's office space was located in the suburbs. The suburbanization of employment moves work away from inner-city residents, which means that those who need jobs the most are literally farthest away from them. Without automobiles, and stymied by public transportation designed to take commuters into cities rather than in the other direction, many inner-city residents depend on public assistance because they cannot get to work.[30]

Collectively, suburbs wield real power. They are where most Americans live, and since 1975, their representatives constitute the largest voting bloc in Congress. Individually, they shape their own demographies because they are minigovernments. By world standards, these small communities possess extraordinary capacities to define land use, organize institutions, and tax residents. Because so many services are financed in whole or in part by local property taxes, the economic disparity among suburban tax bases and between suburbs and cities translates into dramatic inequalities. In 1997–98, for instance, the four counties surrounding Philadelphia spent an average of $1,900 more per pupil for schooling than the city did. As suburbs hoard their resources, shielding them from cities, they become central agents in the reproduction of segregation and poverty in America. The invisible walls suburbs erect to keep poor people within city limits concentrate poverty and increase the burdens on the welfare state, while suburban legislators wield their political power to reduce the public benefits that their exclusiveness helped make more necessary.[31]

Suburbs are not nearly as independent of cities as their residents think, however, and a growing body of literature traces the economic links that join them. "To compete in the global economy," argues the Department of Urban Housing and Development's *State of the Cities, 1998* report, "cities and their suburbs must cooperate more than they compete." Metropolitan economies depend on "urban strengths and have a huge stake in city job growth."[32] Cities and suburbs blend in other ways as well. With the advent of the downtown shopping mall, suburban architectural and retail forms have come to central cities, where they have hastened the privatization and control of public space. Meanwhile, the city's problems have infiltrated the suburbs with traffic congestion, aging infrastructure, strained finances, and even increased poverty. As central city and suburb increasingly turn toward each other, the differences between them blur. Affluent suburbanites may pick up stakes and move farther outward, but they cannot avoid this process forever, or even for long. Nor are suburbs independent of the welfare state. Suburbanites are laid off from their jobs and lose their benefits. They worry about paying for their parents in nursing homes. They try to imagine how they will keep their standard of living in retirement. As American suburbanites face these problems, they find themselves as dependent on the welfare state as a single mother in the inner city.

Americans migrated south and west as well as to the suburbs. Together, federal government spending, economic opportunity, and an appealing lifestyle fueled explosive job growth and urban development in the region south of the thirty-seventh parallel, stretching from the Carolinas to Silicon Valley. The Sunbelt, the name given to this new region, captured the glamour and the sense of possibility in the nation's reordered urban hierarchy.[33]

The American mobilization for World War II accelerated the Sunbelt's development. Between 1940 and 1943, expanded defense production and huge military facilities pumped money, jobs, and infrastructure into the region and tilted the national economy toward the southern Atlantic, Gulf, and Pacific coasts. After the war, the federal government nourished Sunbelt growth with about 60 percent of the military budget and a disproportionate share of defense production facilities and military bases. It also located more civilian jobs in the Sunbelt than elsewhere. The Sunbelt states offered less expensive labor and other operating costs, fewer unions, and more Republican votes. When population growth strained the resources of Sunbelt cities, the federal government responded with grants for infrastructure construction, such as highways, water and sewage plants, and mass transit. Federal urban renewal money helped reconstruct aging downtowns. There is a delicious irony in the conservative, antigovernment, antiwelfare politics of a region dependent upon federal spending for its growth and prosperity.[34]

Another irony is this: the federal government increased the attractiveness of the Sunbelt as a place to live, work, and invest by imposing unwanted change on the region. By forcing southern cities to desegregate public facilities and honor the civil rights of African Americans, the federal government helped them to shed their image as centers of racial bigotry, which moderate southern politicians and business leaders realized detracted from the South's appeal.[35]

Consequently, Sunbelt cities grew at an astonishing pace. In the 1960s, 62 percent of the nation's metropolitan growth occurred in the South and West; in the 1970s, the proportion rose to 96 percent. In the 1970s, while the North lost 60.1 jobs for every thousand population, the South gained 92.1 and the West 128.4.[36] This population boom tipped the balance of national political power toward the Sunbelt, thereby reducing political support for welfare state programs, such as public assistance, that did not serve the middle class and elderly.

In some ways, Sunbelt cities gained disproportionately from the increasing importance of foreign trade in the American economy. By 1975, nearly two-thirds of American trade entered or left through West Coast, Gulf, or southern Atlantic ports. Tourism is harder to measure, but self-reporting by Sunbelt states lists it often as the second or third largest industry.[37] Retirees also promoted the fortunes of Sunbelt cities. Census data show large increases in the number of residents over the age of sixty-five in southern and western states, and the flow of their Social Security and Medicare dollars links the health of Sunbelt economies to the welfare state.

In the decades after the war, the progrowth coalitions that controlled Sunbelt cities attracted investment with cheap nonunion labor, low taxes, and limited social welfare spending, as well as minimal zoning, land-use regulation, and building codes. Houston, for instance, spent $1.16 per capita on public welfare in 1970, compared to $9.09 in Chicago; Phoenix spent five cents, compared to $31.90 in Newark. As a result, many Sunbelt cities had underdeveloped social services and shoddy public facilities and infrastructure. Nor did urban prosperity translate into greater income equality. Indeed, poverty was widespread within the region's cities.[38] Nevertheless, major Sunbelt cities of the 1960s and 1970s offered a stunning contrast to the old industrial cities of the North and Midwest. With their booming economies, mushrooming populations, and thriving downtowns, they seemed poised for a golden future—new engines of American prosperity and new sites for the realization of American dreams.

But the 1980s held a different fate for Sunbelt cities. Population figures from 1980 to 1984 showed a sharp reduction in growth. Whereas in the 1970s the number of high-poverty census tracts in the South and Southwest had declined, in the 1980s, with the collapse of oil prices and the shock of the savings and loan debacle, they increased. Sunbelt cities now confronted deteriorating infrastructure, strained municipal resources, corporate downsizing, defense industry reductions, and increased poverty, homelessness, and crime—many of the same issues that were forcing cities in the Rustbelt to develop new strategies for growth and to redefine their social obligations. As with the suburb and the city, the economies and problems of Sunbelt and Rustbelt have been converging. The two regional faces of the new American city increasingly dissolve into one: Sorkin's "ageographical" city, where location collapses into irrelevance and is replaced by the office towers, malls, fast-food restaurants, festival markets, and international airports of the new American city.[39]

Sunbelt and Rustbelt cities also share another defining feature of American urbanism: racial segregation. In American cities, racial segregation—or "American apartheid," in the words of Douglas Massey and Nancy Denton—has not only persisted, but grown. The segregation of African Americans differed fundamentally from the experience of white immigrants from Europe in the nineteenth and early-twentieth centuries. Immigrants never lived in enclaves as ethnically homogeneous as the black ghettos of post–World War II America. And immigrant ghettos did not prove to be permanent. Indexes of segregation and spatial isolation among European immigrant groups declined rapidly after 1910 as economic mobility increased and the native-born children of immigrants moved away from the neighborhoods of their parents.[40]

By contrast, the segregation of African Americans survives at extraordinary levels throughout the nation, although it is generally a little worse in the North and in larger, more modern cities. It is much higher now than in 1860 or 1910. In 1930, in northern cities, except for Chicago and Cleveland, the average African American lived in a neighborhood dominated by whites; by 1970, this was totally reversed, and blacks in all northern cities lived far more often with other African Americans than with whites. The average African American in major northern cities lived in a neighborhood that rocketed from 31.7 percent black in 1930 to 73.5 percent in 1970.[41]

Although it is often equated with poverty, racial segregation afflicts affluent as well as poor African Americans. Indexes of segregation remain about as high for them as for poor blacks. In northern metropolitan areas, the degree of segregation for African Americans with annual incomes of less than $2,500 was the same as for those with incomes of $50,000 or more in 1980. According to Massey and Denton, one of every three African Americans in sixteen metropolitan areas was living under conditions of intense racial segregation they call "hypersegregation."[42]

By no means does segregation signify uniform poverty, run-down housing, or trash-strewn streets. Tidy, well-kept blocks of single-family homes populate the black as well as the white districts of metropolitan America. But the failure of social scientists to document the spaces and neighborhoods of black America has unwittingly reinforced this stereotype, which is sustained by the media, by politicians, and by the unwillingness of most nonblack Americans to acquaint themselves firsthand with the facts. Even so, as Massey and Denton show, segregation by itself can initiate a vicious process that concentrates poverty and intensifies its impact, and by concentrating poverty, segregation vastly increases the burdens on America's welfare state.[43]

All levels of government share responsibility for perpetuating and intensifying racial segregation. In the 1930s the underwriting practices of federal agencies ruined central city housing markets, denied mortgage money to blacks, and promoted the development of white suburbs. Governments used road and highway construction to manipulate or confine racial concentrations. The first federal public housing regulations in the 1930s permitted no project to disturb the "neighborhood composition guideline"—that is, the racial status quo. As a result, before World War II, two-thirds of all public housing with black occupants remained wholly segregated. After the war, local governments used public housing to segregate blacks even more completely.[44]

In addition to racial segregation, economic segregation, which exists independently of race, has also increased among African Americans—as well as among whites and Hispanics in cities of all sizes across the nation. The economic segregation of whites grew most in the 1970s, as deindustrialization and rising income inequality left poor whites concentrated in urban neighborhoods. Blacks and Hispanics caught up in the 1980s. Together with racial segregation, economic segregation mapped the processes that have shaped the new American city and created a new geography of public assistance. Another of these processes was urban redevelopment.[45]

Unless land is vacant, reconfiguring urban space cannot be a benign process. There are people, businesses, and institutions to be moved out, buildings to be demolished, trees to be uprooted. Displacement rarely operates in a socially neutral way: those forced out are disproportionately poor or working class. They appear to be making marginal and unproductive use of valuable land; sometimes, because of their poverty, lifestyle, or race, they seem a nuisance. This process of displacement has a long history. Nineteenth- and early-twentieth-century housing reformers, for instance, wrote about slums, not ghettos, and in both New York City and Philadelphia settlement houses—bastions of reform—played an active part in slum clearance. Along with business and real estate interests, they saw slum clearance not only as the path to better housing for the poor but as the key to developing cities by putting valuable land to more productive uses.[46]

After World War II, slum clearance acquired a new name: urban redevelopment. Real estate interests wanted to use downtown land for development; institutions wanted the room to expand; politicians wanted city growth. Unlike their predecessors, this postwar growth coalition relied on the federal government for help. As a shorthand for the problem they planned to attack, politicians and commentators began to refer to "blight," which became the reigning metaphor for urban distress during the 1940s and 1950s. Growth coalitions stressed the elimination of blight with revived downtowns full of new offices and residences for the well-to-do. Housing for the poor played a subsidiary role in their plans. As in the nineteenth and early-twentieth centuries, reformers who wanted to sweep away slums and their denizens seem to have given remarkably little thought to one important question: where would displaced people go?[47]

With only a few exceptions, public authorities in America did not build housing before the Great Depression of the 1930s. Although the absence of public housing increased the hardships of the poor, the ill housed, and families displaced by slum clearance, most reformers and public officials resisted constructing public housing for a very long time. Only the terrible housing crisis of the Great Depression overcame their reluctance to interfere with real estate markets and their fear of socialism. In 1937, Congress authorized the construction of the first federal public housing. Bitterly opposed by the real estate industry, the legislation did not produce much housing, but it did set a precedent for federal action in public housing.[48]

Congress assumed that public housing should serve only those families too poor to find shelter in the private market, but setting strict income limits, which seemed fair to liberals concerned with distributing scarce resources, had unfortunate consequences. For twenty-five years the nation's major housing program was unable to serve one group of people with real housing needs—the working poor. It also penalized public housing tenants for modest upward economic mobility by evicting them when their incomes rose above an arbitrary ceiling. Eviction often worsened their financial condition and robbed housing projects of stable community leaders. (Finally, in the late 1990s, federal policy makers began trying to modify the income mix among public housing tenants.)[49]

In 1949 the Taft-Ellender-Wagner Housing Act, long sought by housing reformers, set an unprecedented goal for the American welfare state: "a decent home and suitable living environment" for every American family. The act committed federal funds for use by local redevelopment agencies to acquire and redevelop sites. It required that sites be predominantly residential either before or after redevelopment and gave redevelopment agencies the authority to level residential areas labeled slums and replace them with offices, housing, shopping areas, and parking lots. The law also authorized the building of 801,000 public housing units in the next six years and mandated the relocation of displaced families in equivalent housing. The jubilation of housing reformers, however, did not last long. In 1951, New York City's master developer Robert Moses showed how the law could be manipulated to leverage $26 million of federal money to build a coliseum and luxury apartments. By 1952, only 85,000 units of public housing were under construction; eventually, only one-quarter of the authorized housing was actually built.[50]

In the more conservative Eisenhower years, Congress weakened the already fragile link between redevelopment and housing by eliminating the requirement for residential housing in some portions of redeveloped areas. It also introduced the term *urban renewal*, which earned its epithet "Negro removal" by destroying African American neighborhoods. By 1967, urban renewal had replaced 404,000 dwelling units, most of them occupied by low-income residents, with 41,580 units—only 10 percent of the original number, located primarily in racially segregated highrise public housing towers. For the most part shoddily constructed warehouses for the poor, this early public housing reflected the inability of architects and planners to foresee the drawbacks of high-rise living for impoverished families or the social consequences of segregation and concentrated poverty.[51]

If segregated public housing was the ugliest face of urban redevelopment, gentrification was its prettiest. Gentrification—"the rehabilitation of working-class and derelict housing and the consequent transformation of an area into a middle-class neighborhood," as two scholars defined it—not only renovated houses and transformed cityscapes, it also brought a remarkably uniform population to central cities: young, white, childless urbanites with professional or managerial jobs and above-average incomes. (It is a myth that gentrification attracts many suburbanites back to cities.)[52] Gentrification was the residential arm of urban revitalization, paralleling efforts to bring corporate offices, business services, retailing, and tourism back to city centers. Like other forms of redevelopment, it necessitated the cooperation of local elites with city, state, and federal governments. They cooperated because it served all their interests well. Local governments benefited directly because gentrification raised the taxable value of property, attracted affluent consumers who circulated income through local economies, enhanced tourism, and helped hold corporations in central cities. Financial, real estate, and business interests gained in many ways—from commissions on increased transactions, speculation in land and buildings, higher rents, mortgage interest and loans, retail sales, and entertainment spending. Urban professionals profited from attractive housing that suited their lifestyle. Nonetheless, gentrification produced losers as well as winners—most often the poor, displaced by gentrification, facing steeper rents in tight real estate markets.[53]

Conversely, large urban districts often deteriorated because they were pushed outside the market, and poor people found themselves homeless in a sea of abandoned housing. Declining real estate values and the inability of poor people to pay high rents made much inner-city residential real estate unprofitable—unappealing to landlords, unresponsive to market-based public policies, and dependent for improvement or development on infusions of capital from government, philanthropy, or local community economic development strategies.[54]

In the early 1980s urban social critics linked abandonment and gentrification as complementary phases in the history of urban land markets and capital accumulation. For urban planner Peter Marcuse, the twin processes gave geographic form to the economic polarization of the city. They created a "vicious circle . . . in which the poor are continuously under pressure of displacement and the well-to-do continuously seek to wall themselves . . . within gentrified neighborhoods." The effect of displacement from abandonment and gentrification is not trivial. In New York City in the early 1980s Marcuse estimated displacement from abandonment at 60,000 households, or 150,000 people each year. He put annual displacement from gentrification, which is harder to measure, at 10,000 to 40,000 households. Total annual displacement in the United States has been estimated at 2.5 million persons.[55]

In the mid-1980s, homelessness, one consequence of displacement, suddenly surfaced as a public issue. Rising joblessness, increased poverty, the destruction of cheap lodging in skid rows, and the deinstitutionalization of the mentally ill rank high among the factors that have inscribed homelessness into urban landscapes. Homelessness often originates in neighborhoods marked by poverty, unemployment, abandoned housing, overcrowding, female-headed families with young children, and few social and family supports—the neighborhoods created by the great transformations of urban economy, demography, and space.[56]

Another powerful force in the transformation of public and private space was highway construction. When its full history is written, highway construction may emerge as even more destructive than urban renewal. Major federal support of highways resulted from two federal laws passed by Congress in 1956, which fixed the federal contribution to the cost of interstate highways at 90 percent, to be financed through gasoline taxes. Ten times more expensive than urban renewal, new highways were supposed to help cities by channeling traffic downtown; instead, they spurred the growth of suburbs. They also caused massive displacement; whole districts had to be leveled to accommodate roadways and interchanges. Congress did not require local or federal authorities to find housing for the mainly low-income families whose homes were to be destroyed. "Black communities," writes historian Raymond Mohl, "were uprooted in virtually every big city to make way for the new urban traffic arteries." The path of construction did not run through poor and black neighborhoods by chance. Often, local authorities, fixated on remaking downtowns, wanted to wipe out poor neighborhoods or to use highways as barriers between these neighborhoods and the redeveloping sections of their cities.[57]

Urban redevelopment and highway construction altered the physical appearance of American cities and cut the templates for future downtown development. They built an urban infrastructure for the emergent world economy of the information age and formalized mechanisms for turning the always mixed public/private economy of urban development into a major force for the reconstruction of cities. As a result of federal housing initiatives, the amount of substandard housing decreased, especially during the Great Society, when Congress greatly expanded federal construction of public housing and authorized money for housing rehabilitation and rent supplements.[58] Nonetheless, urban redevelopment and highway construction also hastened the deterioration of local neighborhoods and fueled a new social geography of public assistance based on the concentration of poverty into large, racially segregated, and isolated districts where residents lived in substandard housing or the new postwar public housing slums. The office tower and the high-rise public housing project are both products of post–World War II urban redevelopment, and they are linked causally, not accidentally.

. . . .

The new American city dazzles with its wealth and opulence. Count the expensive restaurants; watch the shoppers in the exclusive stores; look at the price of real estate and the high rents. But the new American city also depresses with its poverty. Step over the homeless men and women sleeping on grates; avoid the beggars; drive through neighborhoods of abandoned or neglected housing; look at the men and women lined up for shelters or free food. Income inequality and poverty worsened between the early 1970s and the early 1990s and hardly budged thereafter. More people are poor; the geographic concentration of poverty in cities is greater than ever before; poor people lead more isolated lives. By the 1990s, this concentrated poverty had spread to cities across the nation, from Rustbelt to Sunbelt.

Mike Davis calls Los Angeles, emblematic for him of the new American city, "fortress L.A." Security dominates urban design in its privatized spaces. Active life takes place away from the streets. Underground passages, skyways, and malls—private spaces where beggars can be barred, unpleasant or threatening encounters avoided, and movement monitored with video cameras—assure workers and shoppers minimal contact with the rougher, unpredictable, uncontrollable diversity of the streets.[59]

Fortress America was built on fear—the belief that crime, violence, and danger stalked the city. Until recent decades, urban architecture exuded a confidence incompatible with deep concerns about crime: stores opened directly onto public streets, homes and buildings could be entered with little difficulty, and schools had several entrances, which remained unlocked. At the beginning of the twenty-first century, this earlier urban architecture seems naïve, and retrofitting older homes and buildings with security systems, stronger locks, and window bars has become a minor urban industry.

There are as many anecdotes about urban crime as there are people who live in cities. Everyone has a story, if not about his or her own mugging or break-in, then about a friend's or neighbor's. City people feel besieged; crime dominates talk at dinner parties as well as on the nightly news. Although trends in crime do not conform to popular beliefs— crime rates dropped dramatically in most cities in the middle and late 1990s, for example—it is perception that has fueled the construction of Fortress America.

Crime opens a window on how the great transformations in urban economy, demography, and space register in the daily lives of people in cities. It embodies the translation of poverty, hopelessness, and frustration into rage; it records the acting out of blocked aspirations in robbery; it traces the consequences of low wages and joblessness in drug dealing. It follows heightened poverty and inequality as they arc back toward the affluent in the form of street mugging, burgled homes, and smashed windshields. It maps the consequences of urban redevelopment that have turned city centers into places of danger by leaving them devoid of activity after dark. In 1961 urban critic Jane Jacobs described the conditions for safe and healthy city streets—multiage dwellings, density, short blocks, mixed uses of space. Her book created a sensation, but mainstream urban redevelopment ignored its prescription, and the statistics of urban crime reflect the results.[60]

The gleaming corporate complexes transforming downtowns encase the heart of the new American city in glass, steel, and concrete. However, even cities that negotiated economic transition with some success have not avoided the problems of Camden or East St. Louis. Rather, the new urbanism has superimposed a social geography, architecture, economy, and lifestyle on top of deteriorated neighborhoods, concentrated poverty, and economic redundance. The architecture of downtown faces forward, toward the global city; the architecture of poor and modest neighborhoods faces backward, toward the defunct industrial city.

The privileges of wealth—private guards, expensive security systems, secure buildings, isolation from the street—separate redeveloped downtowns and rich residential districts from poorer neighborhoods that cannot afford the price of safety. Wealth also buys cleanliness and well-maintained streets. Downtown businesses and property owners, as in Philadelphia and New York City, organize and pay for their own special service districts, whose employees clean and monitor the streets.

Inner-city neighborhoods, by contrast, show no signs of privilege. Despite the occasional modern school, hospital, prison, or housing project, most buildings date from earlier eras. Once-gracious homes of the upper-middle class trace white flight and increased poverty in their neglect and multiple mailboxes. Vacant buildings, pawn shops, check-cashing agencies, and struggling small businesses populate the old stores in now depressed blocks of formerly vibrant neighborhood shopping districts. Trash-filled streets signify the poverty of city governments unable to pay for their cleaning and the inability of residents to hire private services. Weeds surround the broken benches in local parks.

It is easy to leave the study of recent urban history overwhelmed by a sense of inevitability and despair. But there are antidotes to nihilism. Everywhere, modest but hopeful signs appear. A new grass-roots politics of community development has scored significant victories. Exciting examples of urban revitalization exist in cities around the country. Some indications of distress, notably poverty rates and unemployment, have leveled off or declined a bit. Cities remain vibrant centers of arts, culture, education, and research, and the new immigration has rekindled the diversity that lies at the core of the urban experience and constitutes its great appeal.[61]

Policy options, it is crucial to remember, always exist. The new American city emerged as the result of political choices as well as great impersonal forces. It represents human agency as well as structural transformation, and it embodies decisions made at every stage of its construction. The existence of urban alternatives—of the possibility of different urban outcomes even in the modern era—abound in Canada and Europe. Unfortunately, the coalitions that guided urban reconstruction in the United States chose paths that favored large commercial and real estate interests and disadvantaged poor and minority residents. The contradictions inherent in their strategies furthered the deterioration of vast stretches of inner cities, increased racial segregation, intensified poverty, and created huge problems for the welfare state, which inherited the responsibility for responding to the human consequences of the new American city. There is no reason why the same choices must be repeated now and in the future.

3

THE FAMILY SUPPORT ACT
AND THE ILLUSION
OF WELFARE REFORM

With the right turn in American politics, federal and state government efforts to reform welfare in the 1980s did not attempt to reverse the trends in poverty, inequality, and joblessness associated with the new American city. Instead of leading a new charge against poverty and its causes, they focused on trimming the number of people on welfare and cutting benefits, a crusade against "dependence"—in particular, the reliance of young unmarried mothers on AFDC and the pittance provided by the remaining state public assistance programs.

To be sure, AFDC did need reform. A host of counterproductive regulations, together with the absence of child care and medical insurance for clients who left the rolls, worked against moving AFDC recipients from welfare to work. Strict limits on the assets that clients were allowed to retain in order to receive benefits—such as the value of a car or any appreciable saving—meant that many could not reach jobs, save for emergencies, or acquire the modest capital necessary to buy a house or start a small business. And the steep reduction in benefits that followed from almost any earned income discouraged clients from taking jobs to supplement their welfare benefits. Because former AFDC clients usually took low-wage jobs without benefits, "independence" meant the loss of medical insurance and the inability to afford medical care. In addition to these practical considerations, conservatives complained that benefits carrying neither work requirements nor time limits encouraged long-term dependence. Liberals, on the other hand, objected to low benefits that varied drastically from state to state and to the often punitive and stigmatizing manner in which they were administered. Clients, meanwhile, found the benefits they did receive inadequate and the administrative procedures demeaning.

The Family Support Act of 1988 (FSA) addressed some of these issues. As well as introducing work obligations, the FSA enhanced the collection of child support from noncustodial parents and strengthened federal support for child care, education, and job training as part of public assistance. However, by failing to create jobs or address the inadequacy of wages, the FSA repeated the historic failure of American social policy to link public assistance with labor markets. At most, the FSA promised to reduce the AFDC rolls and increase child support payments; it offered little hope of reducing poverty or promoting lasting economic independence. And even these limited goals were compromised: inadequate federal funding and reluctant state governments prevented any valid test of the FSA's real potential while reliance on positive incentives and supports marked it as an anachronism in the new, punitive, market-directed era of welfare reform.[1]

The FSA looked toward both the past and future of social policy. The first major legislative overhaul of AFDC since the 1930s, it brought together three important strands in the history of public welfare: the centuries-old attack on outdoor relief, the failed search for ways to link welfare to work, and the ineffective struggle to collect child support from noncustodial parents.

Outdoor Relief

The story of American welfare begins in the colonial era with "outdoor relief," for most of the nation's history the common term for what, in America today, is usually called welfare. Outdoor relief consisted of public aid—food, fuel, small amounts of cash—given to needy people outside of institutions. Administered by towns, counties, or parishes, it was one of the earliest responsibilities of American local governments. Dreary, often depressing, outdoor relief remains the least-studied facet of America's welfare history. Nevertheless, in various guises—home relief, General Assistance, AFDC, and now Temporary Assistance for Needy Families (TANF)—outdoor relief has proved to be the bedrock of American welfare. Its persistence shows the crucial need for a government role in the care of needy people throughout America's past and undermines the claim that voluntarism and private charity suffice to meet the needs of people unable to survive on their own.[2]

By the late-eighteenth and early-nineteenth centuries, outdoor relief had surfaced as a major concern of public policy. Immigration, urbanization, and the spread of wage labor increased the number of people unable to care for themselves, especially in cities and large towns. As local and state authorities complained of rising expenses for poor relief, they faced issues familiar in current debates about poverty and welfare. The first enduring question was how to distinguish between those who would receive help and those who would not. Because neither public nor private resources have ever been adequate to relieve all need, government and charities struggle to identify who merits help. Until the second and third decades of the nineteenth century, most commentators talked about drawing a line between the able-bodied and the impotent poor—those who could work and those who could not. In practice, no one could draw such a line with any precision. By the mid-nineteenth century, this old dichotomy had been moralized into the deserving and undeserving, or the worthy and unworthy, poor, and "behavior," in addition to physical condition, had become a criterion for relief.

The second enduring issue was the impact relief might have on work incentives and family life. Critics worried that relief sapped the will to work. Generous relief policies, they believed, lessened the supply of cheap labor and encouraged the formation of a permanent pauper class. The adverse consequences spilled over into family life; the demoralized poor failed to properly train or supervise their children, families disintegrated, and pauperism perpetuated itself across generations. Added to this concern was a third issue: the limits of social obligation. What should communities provide even the deserving poor? What do citizens owe each other? These matters remain as contentious today as they were two hundred years ago.

In the late-colonial period and the early republic, the "settlement" issue complicated definitions of social obligation. Then, the responsibility of a community extended only to its members. Those who belonged to the community—who had a settlement—were entitled to public assistance; others were "warned" out or forcibly driven or transported outside town or county boundaries. Advancing welfare policy beyond the narrow confines of family and community required a moral and theoretical leap—in Michael Ignatieff's phrase, the extension of kindness to strangers. Succeeding generations made this leap reluctantly and imperfectly, and an unwillingness to help those who seem different, alien, or outside a narrow definition of community poses as great an obstacle today to generous social welfare policy as in the days of the old settlement laws.[3]

The poor law reforms of the early-nineteenth century attempted to address many of these problems. The first major initiative was the construction of poorhouses (indoor relief) by state governments. By forcing everyone who wanted relief into poorhouses, they hoped to deter people from applying in the first place. If fewer applied, dependence would be less of a problem, relief would not undermine labor supply, and the costs of assistance would drop.

Poorhouses did not accomplish their purposes. Indeed, they proved much more expensive than outdoor relief, and the number of people seeking relief continued to rise. For decades, poorhouses served many relatively young and able-bodied men as temporary refuges during times of slack work or while they looked for employment. Initially, they also served as orphanages for children and hospitals for the mentally ill. They housed helpless and sick old men, some old women (though women more often lived with their children), and, on occasion, young unmarried pregnant women. They were terrible places—dirty, disorderly, full of disease, with miserable food and accommodation. As the nineteenth century progressed, state governments removed more and more inmates from poorhouses into separate institutions or onto the streets: children, able-bodied men, the mentally ill, the sick. By the early-twentieth century, poorhouses had essentially become public old-age homes.[4]

Moreover, despite the construction of poorhouses and a barrage of criticism from politicians, public officials, and reformers, many more people still received outdoor than indoor relief. And many reformers looked for ways to end or reduce it. The most notable nineteenth-century war on outdoor relief began in Brooklyn, New York, in 1878, when Mayor Seth Lowe persuaded the city council to abolish it. Brooklyn was one of ten of the nation's forty largest cities that did away with public outdoor relief between the late 1870s and the early 1890s; others reduced the amounts provided. But their expectation that private charity could meet the legitimate needs of the worthy poor proved illusory, and they found they could not do without public outdoor relief for long. By the second decade of the twentieth century, even former opponents of outdoor relief recognized it as a necessity, and debate shifted away from its justification to its administration. Whether relief was public or private mattered less than honesty, efficiency, and professional management.

In 1911, another form of outdoor relief arrived when Illinois and Missouri became the first states to offer mothers' pensions, which were small payments to widows. Championed by reformers since the late-nineteenth century, mothers' pensions for the first time made outdoor relief a state as well as local responsibility. By 1919, mothers' pensions existed in thirty-nine states and the territories of Alaska and Hawaii. In 1931, they supported 200,000 children, in every state except Georgia and South Carolina. Even so, their low benefits covered only a fraction of potential recipients, and they required longtime state residence and good behavior as a condition of eligibility. However, despite their limitations, they helped prevent the breakup of many families and represented the first halting step on the road from charity to entitlement.

During the New Deal era, women reformers in the newly created Children's Bureau urged the federalization of mothers' pensions in order to permit deserving women—still mainly widows—to remain at home with their young children rather than work for wages. The Aid to Dependent

Children provision of the Economic Security Act of 1935 resulted from their efforts. At the time, President Franklin Roosevelt did not realize that in ADC his administration had set in motion a major new federal public assistance program, and no one predicted its growth and transformation into what AFDC became.[5]

The New Deal was the first time that the federal government provided outdoor relief. The Federal Emergency Relief Administration (1933) and the Civil Works Administration (1934) were the two major agencies founded for this purpose. At its peak, the Civil Works Administration employed 4.26 million workers, or 22.2 percent of the potential workforce. Combining work with welfare, it was the greatest public works experiment in American history. But President Franklin Roosevelt had authorized federal relief only as an emergency measure to avoid mass starvation and save bankrupt state and local governments; he shared the conventional view that relief eroded the will to work and bred dependence. As soon as he could, he returned the responsibility for outdoor relief to the states. The end of federal relief brought great hardship; many people were left with no money for food, fuel, housing, and—despite a new federal work program, the Works Progress Administration—no job.[6]

While FDR is remembered as the founder of the welfare state, the boldest attempt to transform welfare was proposed by, surprisingly, President Richard Nixon in 1969. His Family Assistance Plan would have introduced a "negative income tax"—a guaranteed minimum income for all. It would have eliminated specific disincentives to work and made unnecessary a welfare bureaucracy to determine eligibility and monitor compliance. It met defeat in Congress, however, where a later reform of outdoor relief similar to Nixon's promoted by President Jimmy Carter was also turned down. After that, the idea of a negative income tax faded as a potential public policy solution despite the fact that dissatisfaction with "welfare" was shared by everyone—conservatives, liberals, and recipients alike.

Even after two centuries of attack on the problem of dependency, in the late 1980s probably a higher proportion of Americans received outdoor relief than at any time other than during the Great Depression. With their goal of reforming outdoor relief—now packaged as AFDC—champions of the Family Support Act confronted a challenge that earlier generations of reformers had consistently failed to meet.[7]

Work Relief

By the early 1980s, an insistence on work as a precondition of benefits joined the concern with dependence to form the core of a "new consensus" about welfare. "People on welfare ought to work, work, work," declaimed Senator William L. Armstrong of Colorado, "because it is good for the soul, because it is fair to the taxpayers, because it rankles people who are paying taxes to support these programs to see people who are recipients not get out and work." This message was reinforced in Lawrence Mead's *Beyond Entitlement,* which argued that permissive government had increased welfare dependence by giving people benefits without requiring them to work. Richard Nathan, a social policy analyst and former federal official, summed up the new consensus in the label "new style workfare": "The operative concept is *mutual obligation,* which combines an obligation on the part of the state to provide services and on the part of recipients to participate in these services." The emphasis on work and the preoccupation with dependence pointed to the same solution: the goal, said Senator Daniel Patrick Moynihan, the Senate's leading expert on poverty and welfare, was to convert welfare from "a permanent or even extended circumstance" to "a transition to employment."[8]

Outside policy circles, however, critics blasted "new style workfare." At best, workfare "would provide opportunities for a handful of welfare recipients," observed political scientist Frances Fox Piven and social critic Barbara Ehrenreich. At worst, it would introduce a "new form of mass peonage that would ultimately be as damaging to society as to the women and children it purports to help." Although without question, "well-funded voluntary programs offering high-quality child care and job training would help," they doubted that the proposed programs would offer either.

The historic record of attempts to join welfare to work also called into doubt the prospects of workfare. Indeed, for two centuries, seemingly intractable contradictions had undermined efforts to use work as a deterrent to relief, to force paupers to contribute to their own support, or to move dependent individuals from public assistance to regular jobs.[9]

In the eighteenth and nineteenth centuries, outdoor relief generally carried no work requirement because it supported mainly women with young children or the elderly and infirm. Nonetheless, the American equation of work with virtue permeated early welfare reform, especially plans for poorhouses, which called for inmates to work—as a deterrent and a test of motivation as well as to build character and defray costs. But most poorhouse superintendents failed to find useful work for inmates, and "idleness," in the language of the day, remained a "great evil." Private charities, meanwhile, often applied work tests to men and teenage boys who asked for relief. When they could, they directed them to jobs, which they expected them to take as a condition of further aid. Women presented a dilemma because they were expected to stay at home with their children. Still, the Charity Organization Societies employed some women in laundries and encouraged others to sew at home or take jobs as housekeepers, which meant cleaning and supervising the tenements in which they lived in exchange for free rent.[10]

It was not until the depression of 1893 that work became a form of public assistance rather than a condition of relief. Faced with unprecedented suffering, cities for the first time developed public works projects—street sweeping, sewer construction, street paving, building construction—as forms of relief, and private associations turned over the money they collected to city governments to spend on creating jobs. Neither the states nor the federal government provided any funds for work relief. And these projects had other limits, too: none outlasted the economic crisis; they reached a minority of those who needed help; and they paid very little. Even so, they met with angry criticism from advocates of scientific charity, who believed such jobs would demoralize the poor, and from businessmen, who objected to government meddling in the labor market.

Thus, a hundred years ago, work relief already confronted a vexing and persisting problem: how to avoid interfering with the private labor market. Used indiscriminately, work relief could steal jobs from employed workers, and low wages could undercut their pay. High work relief wages, on the other hand, could swell the rolls of public assistance and drive up costs by making it too attractive. Wages were only one of the problems that undercut work relief over the years. Others became especially evident in the New Deal's unprecedented and massive work programs, which flourished until World War II briefly eliminated unemployment.[11]

In addition to its early public assistance programs, the New Deal provided federal work relief through the Civilian Conservation Corps and the National Youth Administration as well as the Works Progress Administration, which within a year had put more than 3 million people to work. But despite their many achievements, none of these programs met its goals. The WPA, for instance, reached only a fraction—by one estimate, one-quarter—of the eligible unemployed. Wages paid for work relief failed to lift workers out of poverty or even to provide them with enough money for subsistence. Because the federal government had no employment and training infrastructure in place, at times of crisis it was faced with a choice between developing programs slowly and carefully or responding quickly with inadequately considered improvisations. Moreover, the inconsistent goals of public works programs proved impossible to reconcile. To be useful and efficient, programs needed qualified workers, incentives for good work, and the power to dismiss the incompetent or lazy. But they were also supposed to maximize employment, which meant hiring unskilled workers, offering few incentives, and rarely firing anybody. Workers, for their part, found themselves expected to show gratitude for public generosity by toiling hard while forgoing normal workers' rights, such as collective bargaining or strikes. The question of eligibility further complicated matters. Who needed help most? Every criterion discriminated against somebody. The WPA tried to solve the problem by choosing workers only from relief rolls and limiting employ-ment to one job per family, but its rules hurt the recently unemployed, women, and large families.[12]

For a brief moment during World War II, economic and welfare pol-icy seemed ready to merge in a federal commitment to full employment. As historian Alan Brinkley writes, the work of the National Resources Planning Board, appointed by President Roosevelt to plan for the post-war era, "represented an effort to link the commitment to full employ-ment with the commitment to a generous welfare state." However, conservatives, appalled by its vision of central planning and a generous welfare state, quickly scuttled the NRPB report and forced the board out of existence. To some liberals the Employment Act of 1946, which declared full employment a national goal, appeared to be a second chance to realize the NRPB's objective, but the bill's vague language and subsequent dilution only reinforced the separation of economic goals from welfare policy.[13]

During the 1960s, the federal government tried to link economic growth and welfare reform by experimenting with labor market policy. Officials in the Department of Labor stressed the importance of job training to macro-economic policy; members of Congress argued for the creation of public jobs to supplement work available in the private labor market; Willard Wirtz, secretary of labor, wanted to include "subemployment" among the nation's official employment problems; and President Johnson tried to involve the private sector in public job training. Nonetheless, concluded political scientist Margaret Weir, all this activity "left a surprisingly meager legacy." One reason was that the War on Poverty took precedence over effective training policy and subsumed labor market programs. By the late 1960s, observed Weir, "labor market policies," associated increasingly with African Americans, "had become politically identified as income maintenance policies not much different from welfare."[14]

In 1967, with the Work Incentive Program (WIN)—now known as workfare—the federal government revived work as a precondition of relief. WIN required welfare officials to refer employable AFDC clients to jobs and used incentives—welfare recipients were allowed to keep some of their earnings, for example—to encourage employment. It did not try to reshape labor markets by creating jobs, and it did not train welfare recipients for employment that would help them escape poverty. Like earlier programs, WIN failed. In the program's first twenty months, only 10 percent of the 1.6 million cases referred for work were considered employable. Conservatives criticized WIN for not reducing welfare dependency; liberals objected that it did not lift families out of poverty— only 24 percent of men and 18 percent of women who participated in WIN training found a job when the program ended, and those who did find work earned low wages. Furthermore, WIN did not stop the rapid growth of the AFDC rolls.[15]

In the 1970s, Democrats trying to focus their party position seized on public employment as a cure for joblessness. The result was a new 1973 public-service job creation program, the Comprehensive Employment and Training Act (CETA), which subsumed earlier programs. It emphasized short-term job creation, often for unskilled and semiskilled positions like clerks, typists, guards, and road crews, along with jobs in maintenance, repair, and warehouse work. It did not provide any training, and its critics accused it of favoring individuals capable of finding jobs for themselves rather than those in need of skills. Critics also contended that local governments used CETA funds to pay for existing jobs rather than to create new ones. Administered locally, CETA "bore the earmarks of pork barrel politics."[16] In retrospect, CETA's accomplishments have received less attention than its failures, and yet, especially after Congress revised the program in 1976, its achievements were substantial. For instance, CETA funded community-based organizations like the Opportunities Industrialization Centers; Jobs for Progress/Service, Employment, and Redevelopment; and the National Urban League. It supported many projects for youth, such as experimental programs in the Job Corps (originally part of the Economic Opportunity Act of 1964) and projects designed to rehabilitate young offenders. Most of these projects, which would not have been implemented without CETA's resources, provided useful public services while employing participants from mostly disadvantaged backgrounds, who performed their jobs as well as regular employees. Nonetheless, CETA did not transcend the historic tensions that crippled work relief and public works programs, and it was not part of a comprehensive policy designed to increase economic growth by creating human capital and permanent jobs.[17]

After 1980, the newly ascendant Republicans, responding to supporters who believed that job training programs distorted labor markets and inflated wages, cut the programs to the bone. Not simply "an incremental shift in policy," noted Weir, this decimation signaled a "rejection of the notion that the government could—and should—directly intervene in the economy to ensure adequate employment for its citizens." Federal spending on labor market programs plummeted from $15.6 billion in 1980 to $5 billion in 1985. In 1982, the Reagan administration replaced CETA with the much less costly Job Training Partnership Act, an example of the increasing reliance on the private sector to administer public programs. The JTPA offered more help to employers in search of low-cost labor than it did to potential workers looking for good jobs, and it served women worse than CETA had. Furthermore, its record of job placement was not impressive. From April to June 1987, for example, 45 percent of women and 39 percent of men left the program without finding a job. In Milwaukee, a study found that 51 percent of those who did find employment no longer held the same job three months later.[18] Thus the history of putting welfare recipients to work, which would be a primary objective of the Family Support Act, was far from encouraging.

Child Support

The Family Support Act also emerged partly as a response to the frustration of public officials unable to force absent fathers to support their children. In one way or another, the problem of child support has hovered around questions of relief and welfare throughout American history. No one could cast young children among the undeserving poor, but how to help them without rewarding their dissolute parents or encouraging adult dependence has been an enduring dilemma.

When most women with young children who applied for relief were widows, or when, as was often the case in the nineteenth and early-twentieth centuries, their husbands had been incapacitated by illness or industrial accident, the problem of enforcing support by absent fathers was moot. Women bearing children out of wedlock appear to have been more likely to give them up for adoption than to seek public assistance. Many sought shelter in a maternity home or, if desperate, a poorhouse. A large if indeterminate number placed their children in foundling homes, or "baby farms," where the infants often died.[19]

The great nineteenth-century question about child support revolved around the capacity of poor families to care for and raise their children. From early in the century, some observers connected an alleged rise in juvenile crime and immoral behavior to deficient parenting. Their relentless rhetorical attack on the family life of the urban poor conjured fears that vast numbers of unsocialized youngsters—often with immigrant parents—would overrun American cities. Public schools offered one answer, and public school systems were promoted partly as antidotes to crime, poverty, ignorance, and cultural difference.

But public schools parted children from their parents for only a few hours a day. In many instances, when parents required public assistance or private charity, when they drank too much or let their children run unsupervised in the streets, permanent separation appeared necessary. Parents lost custody of children who were committed to reform schools and became wards of the state. When reformers finally won a long battle to remove children from poorhouses, the result was often to separate them from their parents by moving them into other institutions, like orphanages. In the 1850s, the New York Children's Aid Society became the most famous of the several agencies that shipped children to farm families in the West, even though most of them still had a living parent. In the 1870s, Societies for the Prevention of Cruelty to Children gained quasi-public power to police poor families and separate children from parents they considered neglectful or abusive. And Charity Organization Societies often urged widowed or deserted mothers to place their children in institutions.[20]

In the 1890s, reformers who considered themselves "child savers" began to advocate for the preservation of families. Their efforts to reverse the family separation strategy that dominated public policy and private charity culminated in the first White House Conference on Children in 1909, which endorsed their views. Family preservation carried a high price, however: adequate support for mothers and supervision of families in their homes. Mothers' pensions were one response to the problem of support; juvenile courts and the emergence of social services addressed the need for supervision. Kindergartens and other educational reforms enhanced the public role in socialization. Although the number of children in institutions continued to grow during the early-twentieth century, progressive policy now considered institutions poor alternatives to families, not prime instruments of policy.

As the meaning of "child support" changed, policy debate focused less on the moral and financial capacity of poor families to raise their children and more on capturing financial support from absent parents. This shift reflected demographic and cultural transformations. By the late-nineteenth and early-twentieth centuries, desertion had emerged as a significant problem that impoverished many women. Men often abandoned and then returned to their families; wives, undoubtedly desperate for support, abetted their husbands in this process by taking them back. In New York, when wives wanted to extract support from absent husbands, they could sue them in magistrate's courts, but even when they won, enforcement was difficult. "Between 1890 and 1915, every state in the union," writes historian Michael Willrich, "enacted new laws that made a husband's desertion or failure to support his wife or children a crime, punishable in many locales by imprisonment at hard labor." To enforce the new statues, in the 1910s and early 1920s cities throughout the country introduced "the 'socialized' family court," often called Domestic Relations Courts. After midcentury, other factors added to the problems caused by desertion. Starting in the 1960s, marital separation and divorce rose steeply, and the number of out-of-wedlock births escalated. Meanwhile, the stigma attached to out-of-wedlock births, which had once led women to give up their children, faded. A great many mothers and children were now poor because their husbands and fathers refused to support them, not because these men were incapacitated by illness or dead.[21]

The politics of child support also shifted after midcentury. Until the mid-1970s, the federal government took only a minor role in enforcing child support, which remained the responsibility of state and local governments. In 1950, Winfield Denton, an Indiana congressman, proposed a "runaway pappy" law that proved too harsh for Congress, which instead passed a bill requiring AFDC officials to tell local law enforcement officers of deserting parents among families receiving public assistance. Prosecutors, however, rarely pursued absent fathers. And liberals suspected that such child support legislation harmed single mothers more than it helped them because it gave local authorities the right to deny aid to mothers who allegedly failed to cooperate in the pursuit of absent fathers. Thus, liberals successfully opposed the notification requirements in the courts. Nancy Duff Campbell, a former legal services lawyer, told historian Jonah Edelman, "Although welfare mothers at the time made the argument that they did want this kind of support, there wasn't a lot of sympathy for this paternity and support issue" among welfare rights advocates.[22]

Liberal opposition, however, eventually crumbled, in part because of changes in family demographics. Between 1970 and 1985, the proportion of families headed by women nearly doubled. As a result, nearly a quarter of children under the age of eighteen lived in single-parent families, but only a minority of them received support from absent parents. Clearly, the problem was becoming too widespread and serious to ignore. One Senate aide pointed to another reason that the politics of child support had changed—"because the women's groups latched onto it." Women's organizations viewed child support as a way of helping all women, not just those receiving public assistance. The growing number of women in Congress felt the same way, and child support won favor with politicians from both parties. As Edelman observes, "Liberals [liked it] because stricter child support enforcement would make mothers financially better off; conservatives because financially better-off mothers would be less dependent on welfare; both sides but especially conservatives because unlike every other social program, child support, on balance, brought more money into government coffers than it spent and helped defray welfare costs as a result." Both sides also agreed on principle that absent fathers should support their children.[23]

Nonetheless, variable state standards left awards to judicial discretion, resulting in payments that were far too low to meet children's needs, and only a fraction of noncustodial parents paid anything—an evasion reinforced by the inability of state governments to pursue them across state lines. Congress responded, first, in 1974, with the landmark Child Support Act, which created a federal Office of Child Support Enforcement and required states to open comparable offices. The new legislation also extended federal funding to pay for three-fourths of state expenses for enforcement. In 1980, Congress again strengthened child support provisions and in 1984 added the Child Support Amendments, which required every state to set fixed numerical guidelines for child support awards and to withhold payments from the wages of delinquent parents. Despite the conflicts between constitutional rights, civil liberties, and the mandatory provisions of the law pointed out by liberal critics, the 1984 Child Support Amendments passed with no resistance: 422 to 0 in the House and 94 to 0 in the Senate.[24]

As a result of the 1984 amendments, the amount of child support awards started to increase, although only one-third of single parents received any child support payments, and payments remained too low to make a dent in women's poverty or their dependence on public assistance. Thus, improved child support became a logical, irresistible, and urgent component of welfare reform—one of the main objectives of the Family Support Act and one that helped win its passage.[25]

Women who left welfare for work needed child support of another sort—subsidized care for their children. Even with income supplemented from children's fathers, these women's low wages could rarely pay the going rate for child care. And public officials who wanted to push mothers from welfare to work were unwilling to provide them with the support necessary to remain independent. In America, the history of child welfare is shot through with similar contradictions between rhetorical concern for children and the refusal to fund their welfare. (One of the best historical accounts of public programs for children is aptly titled *Broken Promises*.)[26]

Child care has found itself entangled with welfare policy since the nineteenth century. The first day nurseries, which originated to help poor mothers who needed to go to work, met with hostility from women and men who believed mothers belonged in the home. This ambivalence about the legitimacy of working mothers hobbled the development of child care, which remained unable to shed its association with poverty and welfare. In the early-twentieth century, sponsors of family preservation and mothers' pensions wanted to help poor women to stay out of full-time work; the women who ran the federal government's Children's Bureau were by and large hostile to mothers' employment; and with Aid to Dependent Children, the drafters of the New Deal's Economic Security Act also hoped to help mothers stay at home. The only major break in this attitude toward working mothers before the 1970s came during World War II, when the demands of war required full-time employment from women as well as men.[27]

When massive numbers of married women entered the labor force in the 1970s, pressure built to move mothers from welfare to work. Congress responded in 1974 and 1976 by designating federal money to raise public day-care standards and bring more low-income women into child care jobs. These new child care subsidies were restricted to needy families. However, even this modest start on federal child care support stalled and reversed in the 1980s, when the Reagan administration cut funding. The 1981 budget legislation began to transfer responsibility for child care to the states by bundling funds, which had been cut by 20 percent, into block grants and eliminating requirements for state matching funds.[28]

Other Reagan administration policies made use of the tax system to subsidize child care, which increased the advantages only for middle-class women. Federal legislation allowed individuals to exclude the value of employer-provided child care from their gross income and to shelter pretax income in "flexible spending plans." Employers and proprietors also received tax breaks for providing child care and building facilities. This pattern of support through the tax system bifurcated child care along class lines: only women with taxable incomes benefited from tax breaks, which moved child care into the private market.[29]

Responding to government incentives and increased demand, employer-sponsored child care programs mushroomed, and for-profit firms entered the field. In 1977, 41 percent of child care centers were profit making, mostly small independent operations—but child care soon became a big business as chains and franchises moved into the industry: By 1985, Kinder-Care's 1,040 centers served 100,000 children, and Children's World ran 240 centers in thirteen states. Nonprofit centers expanded as well, while in-home care by relatives declined. During the 1980s, as Sonya Michel observed, a new class-based child care system could be divided into four groups: "Publicly funded centers or family caregivers struggling, with declining resources, to provide child care for poor and low-income children; family child care with a primarily work-ing-class and lower-middle-class clientele; voluntary or proprietary cen-ters for middle-class families; and in-home caregiving by nonrelatives, supplemented by nursery schools, for the well-to-do."[30] For the poor, access to child care was governed by the war on dependence. Only the drive to move mothers from welfare to work justified increasing funds for child care. To this day, child care retains its class structure: it remains an adjunct of welfare reform, not a universal right.[31]

The Family Support Act

Despite widespread disgust with AFDC, welfare reform stalled in the early 1980s, a victim of partisan disagreement and historical inertia. Then, in 1986, a combination of events bumped welfare reform up to a higher priority on the national agenda. First, President Reagan called for reform in his State of the Union message: "In the welfare culture, the breakdown of the family, the most basic support system, has reached cri-sis proportions—in female and child poverty, child abandonment, horri-ble crimes, and deteriorating schools. . . . And we must now escape the spider's web of dependency." Reagan charged the White House Domes-tic Council to present him with a strategy "to meet the financial, educa-tional, social, and safety concerns of poor families" by December 1, 1986. Second, the Democratic capture of the Senate placed Daniel Patrick Moynihan in the chair of the crucial Senate subcommittee in charge of the legislation. And lastly, the cuts in federal funds for public assistance that had increased states' fiscal burdens—as well as unmistakable public antiwelfare sentiment—stimulated governors to form a bipartisan com-mission on welfare reform headed by Governors Bill Clinton of Arkansas and Mike Castle of Delaware.[32]

However, until the results of new welfare-to-work demonstration pro-grams became available, no one had solid evidence that welfare reform—defined as moving AFDC recipients into jobs—could succeed. The Omnibus Budget and Reconciliation Act of 1981 had allowed states more latitude to design such programs, and a number of states had seized the opportunity. None of these programs offered very much job training. Instead, they stressed job search—a cheap way of moving peo-ple quickly off the rolls and into jobs, but one whose long-term benefits were uncertain.[33]

The Manpower Demonstration Research Corporation (MDRC), a nonprofit organization, evaluated these new programs in eleven states to "test what works for disadvantaged welfare families." Summarized in a book by MDRC's president, Judith Gueron, *Reforming Welfare with Work* (1987), the results influenced the design and passage of the Family Support Act. "A major shift in the nation's social policy," later wrote a social scientist who had interviewed the key players in federal welfare reform, "seems to have been shaped largely by research and analysis."[34]

The MDRC studies showed that even programs that offered only modest help with job searches led to gains in employment and income among women (but not men) on AFDC and that the most disadvantaged participants gained most. Cost-benefit analyses argued that programs' gains slightly outweighed their expense. And, according to surveys, most participants did not object to mandatory work requirements. Nonetheless, individual gains were small. Most women earned $150 to $600 a year over their former welfare grants, not counting increased work-related expenses, which left most of the women close to the poverty line; most of the increased earnings came from longer work hours, not higher wages. Although the demonstration programs helped some women leave AFDC, Gueron admitted that they "do not appear to move a large percentage of the welfare caseload out of poverty," and many returned to the welfare rolls. A 1987 General Accounting Office analysis drew a similar conclusion: "Evaluations of the work programs have shown modest positive effects on the earnings and employment of participants. But wages were often insufficient to boost participants off welfare. Thus, programs should not be expected to produce massive reductions in the welfare rolls." And the carrots dangled by workfare proponents—child care, education, medical benefits—remained limited and "vastly underfunded."[35]

Despite the modest results of these demonstration programs, state governors and congressional welfare reformers hailed them as the elusive answer to the dilemma of work relief. For the first time in American history, they proclaimed, welfare recipients had been put to work in the regular labor market. The specific welfare proposals before Congress, however, were hardly supported by the MDRC studies. MDRC had not examined the effect of work requirements on mothers with children between the ages of three and six, a group targeted by the proposed legislation, and the studies had focused on short- rather than long-term recipients, the group whose dependence so alarmed welfare reformers. Skeptics could have just as easily used the MDRC data to argue fairly that the proposed welfare legislation would fail.

Nonetheless, the MDRC results buoyed hopes for welfare reform and helped break the legislative logjam in Congress. Viewed by many in Congress as hard, impartial data, the reports appeared to show that work reduced welfare at a reasonable cost, and they reinforced the idea that "citizens who accepted public money owed a mutual obligation." An official of the National Governors Association claimed, "For the first time, we could characterize reform as an investment." A Senate staff member observed, "It was unique. In all the years I worked on welfare reform, we never had a body of data that showed what worked. Now we had it. And those findings were never contested at any level." MDRC, as a *New York Times* editorial noted, "created the data base that convinced Republicans and Democrats that welfare recipients are willing and capable of working." The MDRC results, widely publicized, did not by themselves recommend specific policies. Rather, according to one reporter, they gave "very solid support to the directions people wanted to go in," and in 1988 they convinced undecided House and Senate members to vote for the Family Support Act.[36]

The first major welfare legislation in decades, the 1988 Family Support Act commanded strong bipartisan support, passing the House 347 to 53 and the Senate 96 to 1. Nonetheless, sharp divisions had separated the contending proposals for welfare reform, and the final bill reflected compromise as much as consensus. Republicans and Democrats reached agreement most easily on enhanced enforcement of child support. More controversy surrounded the new state employment and training program (called JOBS) intended to move AFDC clients from welfare to work. "Created as an alternative to mandatory work," observed one analyst, "JOBS became a new (if only partially funded) entitlement to education and training grafted onto an existing entitlement to cash assistance." Although the bill allowed states to design their own programs, it required all of them to offer education, job skills training, and job placement, and it called for 55 percent of JOBS funds to be spent on clients who were already, or were likely to become, long-term AFDC recipients. One of the bill's most contested provisions required clients with children under three years old to participate in JOBS. The bill attempted to facilitate the transition to work through active case management and by extending one year of Medicaid and child care benefits to families who left AFDC for employment.[37]

Congressional conservatives contested the legislation's mandatory extension of AFDC-Unemployed Parents (AFDC-UP) to all states. Introduced in 1961 and made permanent but not mandatory in 1962, the program had allowed states to offer AFDC to two-parent families when the "principal earner" was unemployed. By 1988, only a minority of states participated in the program. As their price for making federal public assistance universal, conservatives exacted a stricter work requirement for unemployed than for single parents. They also prevented the adoption of a national standard for AFDC, whose benefits continued to vary greatly from state to state.[38]

The national press hailed the FSA's passage. "Striving to break a cycle of dependency," proclaimed the *New York Times*, "the Senate today approved the first major revision of the welfare laws since their enactment in 1935." The *Washington Post* praised the FSA as a "landmark overhaul of the welfare system"; the *Los Angeles Times* called it the "most sweeping revision of the nation's principal welfare program—Aid to Families with Dependent Children—since it was created in 1935."[39]

In reality, the FSA offered little hope of reforming welfare, at least in the short run. As two early critics pointed out, it rested on unrealistic assumptions about the availability of good jobs for welfare clients. Most jobs open to low-skilled workers with limited education, a group that included a large share of AFDC clients, did not pay enough to lift a family out of poverty, were frequently insecure, and offered few fringe benefits or opportunities for upward mobility. With the flight of industry from cities, the suburbanization of work, the increase of subcontracting, and the impact of foreign competition and automation, good, long-lasting jobs had become scarce. Nor did workfare—working off welfare payments through employment—open a path to unsubsidized jobs and independence. Employers usually offered only minimal training and support to employees hired through workfare, which itself carried a stigma that made jobs in the regular labor market harder to find. The Family Support Act, predicted another knowledgeable critic, would shuffle people into dead-end jobs in shrinking sectors of the labor market. "Requiring people to work without preparing them for long-term employment will, in the long run, fulfill the worst expectations of welfare reform."[40]

The Family Support Act did enhance child support. It forced women to identify the fathers of their children as a condition of receiving public assistance, set legislative guidelines for awards, and required employers to withhold child support payments from the paychecks of absent fathers. However, the rise in out-of-wedlock births outstripped the increase in the number of awards against unmarried fathers. Although the 1997 share of single mothers receiving support, 31 percent, had risen only slightly in two decades, this overall statistic masked an important change. Among never-married mothers support increased more than four times, from 4 percent to 18 percent, while among previously married mothers it rose from 36 percent to 42 percent. Because state implementation of child support policies varied from state to state, the likelihood that a mother would receive child support still depended very much on where she lived.[41]

. . . .

It is a mistake to judge the intent of social policy solely by the rhetoric of reformers, legislators, or public officials—the real priorities and goals emerge from the study and comparison of budgets. Where, then, have government and private philanthropy been willing to put their resources? For the most part, not in innovative social policies and institutions. For all the talk in praise of work, Congress has never funded work programs adequately. CETA received funds sufficient to employ only about one in twenty of the unemployed, or one in ten of the working poor, and Congress provided its successor program with 70 percent less money. By 1988, funding for WIN, or workfare, had dropped to less than one-third its 1980 level.[42]

The FSA—severely underfunded by Congress—was no exception, although it could claim some accomplishments: improved mechanisms for collecting child support, the extension of AFDC to two-parent families in a number of states, the movement of a small number of clients off AFDC, and the encouragement of state demonstrations of "welfare reform." Nonetheless, doubts that it could meet its goals proved accurate. In contrast to the federal fanfare, states gave the Family Support Act a low-key reception. More progressive states used it to reinforce initiatives already under way. Others proceeded more slowly and reluctantly. By and large, states followed the letter rather than the spirit of the law. They did not, for example, strengthen "mutual obligations" by forcing welfare recipients to work. Mandatory participation, the source of so much public controversy during the bill's passage, proved moot in practice: with state programs reaching only a small fraction of AFDC clients, most participants remained volunteers. The failures of the FSA did not surprise badly paid state social workers, who experienced firsthand the problems caused by too little money for education and training, too few job opportunities, and caseloads that were too high. Rarely could they offer the personalized case management called for by the law.[43]

Money aside, the FSA foundered on the historic separation of welfare from the labor market in American social policy. Sponsors of the FSA assumed that jobs would be available to AFDC clients. They did not want to create jobs, and they permitted state welfare departments to design programs without serious analyses of local labor markets or consultation with labor departments. At a time of declining real wages and fringe benefits, they asserted that after one year, former welfare clients would support themselves—and pay for child care and health insurance—through work. The research with which they justified their claims supported none of these assumptions.

By 1995, the federal and state governments, reported economist Norton Grubb, operated a "bewildering array" of job training programs that cost more than $20 billion each year. What was the result? Grubb put it this way: "The gains in employment and earnings are quite small from a practical standpoint: they are insufficient to move individuals out of poverty or off welfare; their effects very often decay over time, so that even the small benefits are short lived; and, as they are currently constructed, they do not give individuals a chance at middle class occupations or incomes."[44]

The Family Support Act did not improve on this history or revolutionize AFDC. What undermined it, ultimately, was a shift in the welfare debate. By every indication, public sentiment had turned harsher and more punitive. The point was to cut benefits, not extend them. Women should be chased off AFDC with sanctions, not lured away with incentives and new supports. The new benefits, moreover, reflected an out-of-date paternalism, a failed liberal reliance on big government, rather than on the market principles already being applied in state and city government, the nonprofit sector, and the private welfare state.

The FSA strengthened the federal role at the moment when state governments had begun to clamor for more independence and authority. In 1986, an official of the Reagan administration, Charles Hobbs, had proposed to reform AFDC through block grants to the states. Although his recommendations were rejected, he had seen the future. By the 1990s, the initiative in welfare reform had shifted to the states. On the day it was passed, the FSA was already an anachronism.[45]

4

GOVERNORS AS WELFARE
REFORMERS

In the 1990s, state governors proved to be the most aggressive welfare reformers. It was pressure from the governors, in fact, that had broken the congressional welfare logjam in 1988 and paved the way for passage of the Family Support Act. When the FSA failed to transform welfare, states took it upon themselves to cut benefits, change regulations, and experiment with new programs. The governors radically restructured AFDC and Medicaid, trimmed or abolished state assistance programs, and implemented welfare-to-work programs. Although these actions were part of the larger movement to reduce dependence and adopt market models in the welfare state, more than anything else they ushered in a new era in public policy characterized by the devolution of authority from the federal government. The primary leaders within the states were two Republican governors, John Engler of Michigan and Tommy Thompson of Wisconsin.

The Centralization of Social Welfare

The governors claimed they wanted to restore public assistance to its historic and constitutional place in America's federal system. They drew, first, on the Tenth Amendment to the United States Constitution, which reserves powers not granted to the federal government to the states; second, on the tradition of public assistance as a state responsibility throughout the nation's past; and third, on the reputation of states as the pioneering laboratories for innovation during the formative years of American social policy.[1]

Throughout American history the authority over welfare policy had thrust upward toward higher levels of government. The governors proposed to redirect this history of public assistance. From the colonial era until well into the twentieth century, public assistance remained profoundly local. Counties, parishes, towns, and cities developed their own policies toward outdoor relief with increasing but never complete regulation by state governments. As a result, hundreds of local governments administered outdoor relief with a huge variety of rules and benefits.

During the nineteenth century state governments, as we have seen, worked to increase their control of public assistance by curbing the costs of poor relief, revising outmoded settlement laws, and building poorhouses. In New York, the legislature eased some of the burden on local governments by labeling individuals without a settlement (including many immigrants) state paupers and funding their care in poorhouses directly. State governments also opened new institutions to care for the dependent poor: mental hospitals, reform schools, general hospitals, and penitentiaries.[2]

By the close of the Civil War, state governments found themselves supporting a wide array of public and private institutions, which were run with no oversight and accountable to no one. With the dislocation of war, the explosive growth of industry during the Gilded Age, and widespread unemployment resulting from unsteady work and periodic downturns in the economy, the cost of relieving dependence mounted, and the demands for help by institutions and private charities escalated. State governments responded by creating state boards of charities (or bodies with similar names) to collect data and recommend policy. Massachusetts was first in 1863, followed by New York and Ohio in 1867, Illinois in 1869, Pennsylvania in 1870, and other states soon after. Advisory only, sometimes in conflict with local government, these boards lacked executive authority; in 1872, the New York board defined its role as "the moral eye of the State and its adviser in relation to the management of all its eleemosynary institutions."[3]

In the early years of the twentieth century, state governments cautiously innovated in social welfare. They introduced workers' compensation, mothers' pensions, and, in some cases, unemployment insurance, and began to professionalize the administration of public assistance by replacing state boards of charities with departments of public welfare. Expanded and modernized state governments increased their spending in the 1920s. Between 1922 and 1929, per capita state spending, in constant dollars, financed mainly by debt, increased 60 percent. In the same years, cities, starting with Kansas City in 1913, began to create their own public welfare departments and to modernize their administrative procedures.[4]

Any hope that public welfare—or the provision of economic security to all Americans—could remain primarily a state and local function collapsed during the Great Depression of the 1930s. State and local governments facing bankruptcy, unable to turn to private charity, which also was overwhelmed, surrounded by misery, and confronted by militant demands for relief appealed to the federal government for help.[5]

Although President Franklin Roosevelt, as discussed, initially responded with emergency relief—the first federal outdoor relief in American history—followed by a massive program of work relief, it was his Economic Security Act that gave the federal government permanent and unprecedented responsibility for the economic security of the elderly, the unemployed, and dependent children.[6]

The New Deal changed the relationship between the federal government and the states. Under the Constitution, the federal government could not order states to participate in its old age assistance or mothers' aid programs. Instead, it needed to lure state governments with new money. Grants-in-aid, widely used by the federal government for the first time during the 1930s, circumvented the constitutional issue. The federal government did not impose its will on the states; rather, it offered them money they could not afford to refuse, and attached conditions to it. In the process, the New Deal redesigned American federalism. Instead of the constitutional allocation of government functions by level, federalism became a system in which major functions were shared among local, state, and national governments. It is this profound and enduring shift in the nature of federalism that governors in the 1990s tried to modify or reverse.[7]

In the 1930s, the laboratories of policy innovation also moved decisively from the states to the federal government. "The American state is finished," one authority on state government announced. "I do not predict that the states will go, but affirm that they have gone." More accurately, states were the drag retarding progress in public policy. Southern states, intent on preserving cheap labor and a racial caste system, exacted as their price for support of the Economic Security Act the exclusion of agricultural and domestic workers, meaning most blacks, from Social Security. Other states failed to modernize or adequately fund and staff their operations. Even in the early 1960s, state governments still earned the scorn of public policy scholars and professionals who called them the "weak sisters," "fallen arches," and "weakest links" of the federal system.[8]

Thus in the 1960s, the federal government, by necessity, initiated the next great burst of social policy innovations. A private agency, New York City's Mobilization for Youth, funded with Ford Foundation money, and, then, on a larger scale, the President's Committee on Juvenile Delinquency, not state governments, served as laboratories for ideas underpinning the War on Poverty. The poverty war's Community Action Program initially tried to bypass both state and city governments to deliver money directly to new local agencies. Medicare, like Social Security, remained a federally funded and administered program. Meanwhile, Medicaid, a branch of public assistance, followed the AFDC model requiring state matching funds and state administration under federal guidelines. The federal government also directed the most important housing programs, and, of course, it passed the Civil Rights and Voting Rights Acts and enforced desegregation. Progressive changes in social policy, most analysts assumed, could and would issue only from Washington.

Nevertheless, at the height of federal power, state activity in social welfare was still extensive and crucial. States administered and set benefit levels for AFDC and Medicaid, oversaw most federal grant-in-aid programs, and often ran their own General Assistance programs. With major responsibility for public health, even today states outspend federal and local government, operating three times as many hospitals and disbursing two-and-a-half times as much as the federal government on "civilian services" (education, roads, welfare, public health, hospitals, police, sanitation). They contribute 49.8 percent of the cost of elementary and secondary education, compared to 43.8 percent from local and 6.5 percent from the federal government.[9]

A cursory look at a state budget hammers home the magnitude of the contribution. In the late 1990s, the Pennsylvania Department of Public Welfare spent about $5.4 billion out of a total state budget of approximately $17 billion; only spending on education, $6.7 billion, was higher. The department supported about thirty-five services and grant programs, including the county assistance offices, cash grants, county child welfare (which cost nearly $400 million), and homeless assistance. Other departments spent money for social welfare purposes, too. The Department of Education budget included funds for the education of migrant children, the education of indigent children, school-to-work opportunities, and tuition for orphans and children placed in private homes. The Department of Community and Economic Development spent money on housing and redevelopment assistance and on community revitalization. The $200 million budget of the Department of Health included expenditures for maternal and child health, state health care centers, and other programs for low-income families. The Department of Labor and Industry paid for workers' compensation, programs for dislocated workers, and employment services; the Department of Aging funded a variety of social services.[10] Clearly, American welfare remained a state, as much as a national, affair.

The Origins and Early History of Devolution

The history of devolution from the federal to state governments started in the administration of President Richard Nixon. By the time Nixon